ART IN A DESACRALIZED WORLD

Nineteenth Century France and England

Mary R. Anderson

UNIVERSITY PRESS OF AMERICA

LANHAM • NEW YORK • LONDON

University Press of America,™ Inc.

4720 Boston Way
Lanham, MD 20706

3 Henrietta Street
London WC2E 8LU England

Printed in the United States of America

ISBN (Perfect): 0-8191-4148-8
ISBN (Cloth): 0-8191-4147-X

All University Press of America books are produced on acid-free paper which exceeds the minimum standards set by the National Historical Publications and Records Commission.

DEDICATION

For my mother and Diane

and to the memory of my father

ACKNOWLEDGEMENTS

Because this book began as a dissertation at the University of California, Berkeley, it seems entirely fitting to acknowledge first my debt and gratitude to members of that academic community. My thanks belong above all to my dissertation committee: Martin Malia, Martin Jay, and Norman Jacobson. To Martin Malia of the History Department, who directed the original dissertation, my appreciation is deep for the insights which focused and guided my own and for his continuing encouragement. Martin Jay, also of the History Department, though of a philosophical orientation very different from mine, gave the scholar's dispassionate advice throughout the course of the work and a meticulous reading of the text. To Norman Jacobson of the Political Science Department I am grateful both for the depth and pleasure of our conversations and for his careful reading of my work. Any errors and misjudgments are, of course, my own responsibility.

For the generosity of their responses, it is appropriate to mention here the publishing houses of Librairie Ernest Flammarion in Paris for permission to quote Baudelaire's "Correspondances" in its entirety from the 1964 edition of LES FLEURS DU MAL ET AUTRES POÈMES, and William Heinemann Ltd of London in particular for most graciously giving permission to quote from the following poems of Swinburne in the 1924 edition of his COLLECTED POETICAL WORKS: "A Ballad of Death," "A Vision of Spring in Winter," "Time and Life," "Tiresias," "The Higher Pantheism in a Nutshell," "Before a Crucifix," and "Hymn of Man."

To the faculty of Holy Names College, my grateful appreciation is likewise extended, especially to Velma B. Richmond, Dean of Academic Affairs, for her encouragement and support; to Lois MacGillivray, snjm, President, for her interest in promoting this project to its conclusion; to Sister Maureen Patricia McCall, snjm, for the word processing which represents the actual physical conclusion of the work.

To the members of my religious community, the Sisters of the Holy Names, especially Donna Maynard and Michaeline Falvey, my thanks are beyond words for unfailing and loving support.

Faust: If I be quieted with a bed of ease,
Then let that moment be the end of me!
If ever flattering lies of yours can please
And soothe my soul to self-sufficiency,
And make me one of pleasure's devotees,
Then take my soul, for I desire to die:
And that's a wager!

Mephistopheles:
Done!

Faust: And done again!
If to the fleeting hour I say
'Remain, so fair thou art, remain!'
Then bind me with your fatal chain,
For I will perish in that day.

--Johann Wolfgang Goethe, _Faust_,
Part One, Faust's Study (iii)

Faust: Then dared I hail the Moment fleeting,
'Ah, linger still--thou art so fair!'
the traces cannot, of mine earthly being,
in aeons perish: they are there!--
Anticipating here such lofty bliss,
I now enjoy the highest Moment, --this.

Mephistopheles:
No joy can sate him, and suffice no bliss. . .

Faust, Part Two, Act V
(Great Courtyard of the Palace)[1]

TABLE OF CONTENTS

CHAPTER I

INTRODUCTION

"Art for art's sake" is one of the more puzzling features of nineteenth-century European intellectual history, too easily dismissed as an aesthetic cry of revolt against modern society or as a perennial tendency of seekers after dream worlds. Set in its historical context, "l'art pour l'art" (of which Graham Hough understandably once queried "whatever that may mean")[2] becomes a code phrase for something else, an artistic solution to the problem of reordering a desacralized[3] world. The movement functioned both as theodicy and antidote in the post-Christian nineteenth century.

Except for isolated pockets of belief or waves of spiritual enthusiasm which have endured to the present, Christendom as a social reality ceased to exist even before the French Revolution. Whether there was ever a match between popular belief and state usurpation of the Christian churches for state ends or how seriously Christianity has been taken since its social decline are not our concerns here. At the very least, a distinction needs to be made between religious history and ecclesiastical history. What seems clear from the vantage point of one hundred years is that when both the Enlightenment and Romanticism[4] failed to fill the Christian void, the mid-nineteenth century produced a multiplicity of secular religions. "L'art pour l'art" did not completely fill that role. Its function was rather as a theodicy - an artistic justification of various kinds of evil. "L'art pour l'art" justified evil in a world where many denied it or awaited its imminent disappearance. It explained why linear progress cannot exist, why human beings and the societies they create are limited. In defining in a secular way these traditionally religious concerns, "l'art pour l'art" also functioned as an antidote to the theory of progress, in France specifically its St.-Simonian version.[5] The writers we will examine are all representative of the "l'art pour l'art" school, but the range within that school is much greater than has been thought, and all these figures have something to say of art both as theodicy and as antidote. The intent here is to show that, while the theory exhibits certain similarities among all its practitioners, there are many variations, and more important, that the cultural implications of "l'art pour l'art" (though it always remained an elitist phenomenon) run far deeper than providing solace for a coterie in rebellion against society.

Aesthetic revolt is a distinctly modern occurrence and a significant part of the background against which "l'art pour l'art" developed. The role of the artist in the nineteenth century was undeniably different from what it had been in earlier times. Although the newly enfranchised bourgeoisie in France and England probably was not nearly so obtuse as many writers thought, the spread of democracy presented a convenient object of scorn. The existence and new power of the middle classes underlined the fact that the aristocratic literary sponsors of previous centuries no longer existed. In the nineteenth century, literature became subject to the demands of the marketplace, and writers could hardly inveigh as effectively against impersonal economic laws as against a supposed class of parvenus and dilettantes.

The advocates of "l'art pour l'art" often seemed to be defending their artistic egos not merely against the middle classes, but against all the world, an intellectual and emotional possibility created by Romanticism, another of the century's dominant forces. The consciousness of self inherent in Romantic ideas of genius and the artistic ego, personified in Byron and his countless imitators, created a division between claims of self and society. The two often seemed antithetical. Long after Romanticism had become diffused, the self-consciousness it had fostered lived on.

Another nineteenth-century type, the self as man of action, also lived on. From one admittedly narrow perspective, the nineteenth century is preeminently a century of the man of action. The French Revolution of 1789 (and the revolutionary tradition in general) exalted activity over contemplation. The practical man of affairs was frequently juxtaposed with the artistic dreamer, always to the latter's detriment. When writers in France did try to play an influential role, they failed. Between 1830 and 1848 many people in France had looked to their poets for a degree of political leadership. Whether causative or not, the 1848 failure marked a divide between this active period and the general apoliticism of French literary figures in the middle and late century. Added to revolutionary failure was the persistence of St.-Simonian notions of art's social purpose far beyond the utopian sect's dissolution in the 1830's, far indeed beyond the rout of the poets as politicians in 1848. In England the notion of the hero as man of action fused with the society's ideas of utility. Here almost everything seemed reducible to practicality.

Artistic responses to these factors varied. On the one hand, the idea of art as a bearer of social values or as a commodity was summarily rejected, and often society as well. On the other hand, "l'art pour l'art" furnished positive intellectual underpinning for deserting the realm of activity in favor of a new and detached artistic aristocracy. The emphasis on aristocracy also meant that proponents of the theory tended to reject the idea of progress which they thought had produced a bourgeois, democratic world with scant appreciation for art. Nor could progress be applied to artistic production itself. Progress implied perfectibility and manageability, direct threats to the artistic world in which human affairs remain forever untidy and any work of art unrepeatable. For all the advocates of "l'art pour l'art," whatever the variety of their tenets, art simply existed. It need not serve moral, utilitarian, or any purpose at all beyond itself. The intellectual thrust of "l'art pour l'art" thus favored the "otherness" of the exterior world, a position central to modern art.

Alongside these views, art also had an implicit (and generally overlooked) social function for the "l'art pour l'art" advocates in the mid-and late-nineteenth century. For the first time, Western European civilization had become totally and perhaps permanently desacralized, an aspect of the secularization process dating at least from the Renaissance. The centuries following the Renaissance had witnessed the priority of individual experience, a different conception of order based on categories imposed by the human mind rather than discovered in nature as traces of God, an interest in the fact of change itself, and dissolution of the God-world connection which had distinguished Medieval thought. The term "desacralization" adds the dimension that this emerging, secularized, modern society had once seemed sacred. Though Medieval people also had a keen sense of division between "sacred" and "profane," more of everyday life was considered "sacred" than was the case later on. Medieval Christians had celebrated Rogation days in thanksgiving for the harvest or penance for their sins, had learned belief (or beliefs, at any rate) in the stained glass windows of their cathedrals, and seen virtue, vice, and sanctity personified in morality and miracle plays. Even by the seventeenth century, this world was passing into its own kind of mythology. Although there are probably significant differences between the reactions of a Catholic and a Protestant culture to the process of secularization, Christianity in general had previously explained in religious terms limitation, evil, and human folly. The secularization process retained elements of the more Christian past, but it offered as yet no substitute world view to Christianity which would include justifications for these things.

The history of those same centuries since the Renaissance had witnessed, as well, human achievements beyond anything previously known. At least people thought so. The scientific revolution, the Enlightenment, and Romanticism all furthered in their own ways the creation of man as Faust--in Goethe's sense, ambitious, unsatisfied, and insatiable. But catastrophe and limitation continued to exist, and even in the eighteenth century, despite the prevalence of theories of progress, human beings could be exposed as weak after all, often unable to control their own destinies, the possessors even of illusions which are small. No generally accepted explanatory unity like Christianity existed. And by mid-nineteenth century, an anti- Faustian intellectual position, in opposition to the human capabilities suggested by Romanticism and the Enlightenment, became a possibility. The Faust symbol, a highly complicated one, ranges from the traditional anti-Catholic propaganda piece to Goethe's reworking of it. Although there are Romantic and anti-Romantic elements in Goethe's version, it will be considered here from the perspective of Faust as an "ideal type" representing perpetual ambition and insatiable striving. The writers studied here, with one exception, will be considered as types of the anti-Faust, perhaps not a conscious role in their own minds, but one evident from the historian's vantage point, offering an artistic solution to the problem of reordering the desacralized post-Christian world by restoring its intractable evil and pointing up the continued existence of limitation and folly.

We will examine the theory of "l'art pour l'art" as it was established and practiced by five nineteenth-century writers: Charles Baudelaire, Gustave Flaubert, Théophile Gautier, Walter Pater, and Algernon Charles Swinburne. Baudelaire has been chosen because he is perhaps the pivotal figure between the Romantic and modern sensibilities. While sharing Romantic ideas of the poet interpreting and providing access to a sacred realm of mystery, Baudelaire's interest in technique, synesthesia, and the artist's role in society are thoroughly modern. Like Baudelaire, Gustave Flaubert establishes and practices the tenets of "l'art pour l'art," filling his correspondence with elaborations of the theory. Like Baudelaire, too, he is an arch anti-Faust, restoring entire worlds of evil, illusion, and corruptibility.

No study of "l'art pour l'art" could ignore Théophile Gautier, popularizer of the phrase in French letters and during his early career almost the proto-typical artist in revolt against society. Gautier merits serious consideration both for his theories of beauty which imply a private artistic vision and for his reintroduction of the dream world into his own fragmented historical reality. Although Gautier's formulations of "l'art pour l'art" were made earlier in time than Baudelaire's or Flaubert's, he will be examined later here for purposes of our anti-Faustian analogies and because his views were never worked out in equal detail.

Scholars generally support the view that "l'art pour l'art" migrated from France to England.[6] A. C. Swinburne is the major single avenue of that influence. Swinburne's protestations of artistic autonomy in the midst of philistinism read much like Gautier's violent denunciations, though he was more significantly influenced by Baudelaire. Both Swinburne and Walter Pater pushed specific aspects of "l'art pour l'art" to extremes, but their historically grounded differences spring chiefly from the fact that Pater was more aligned to Victorian England than Swinburne. In what he saw as a barbaric and chaotic world, Pater found salvation in art and a center of stillness for the self. For Pater, the sense of human possibilities (though from an essentially spectatorial and interior stance) existed to a greater extent than for Swinburne, the closer imitator of the French school.

All these figures, wherever we find them situated on the spectrum of "l'art pour l'art," have much to say of art both as theodicy and antidote. In a post-Christian time they looked beyond secular religions to the unfinished and ragged parts of the human condition. In a world which too often seemed to exalt progress and possibility, they justified evil and limitation, the intractable and the illusory. Their works illuminate the other face of nineteenth-century humanity, the anti-Faust.

Notes to Chapter I

[1]Johann Wolfgang Goethe, _Faust_, Part One, trans. Philip Wayne (Middlesex, 1975), p. 87. _Faust_, Part Two, trans. Bayard Taylor, rev. and ed. Stuart Atkins (New York, 1962), pp. 222 f.

[2]Graham Hough, _The Last Romantics_ (Oxford, 1961), p. 161.

[3]The phrase is Martin Malia's, used in his nineteenth-century intellectual history classes at the University of California, Berkeley.

[4]The term "Romanticism" is surely among the most complex and ambiguous in historical studies. No attempt will be made here to offer an interpretation of Romanticism as a whole. The term will be used only in reference to specific aspects of the early nineteenth-century Romantic movement, especially its emphasis on human possibilities.

[5]St.-Simonianism derived from the works of Claude-Henri de Rouvroy, Comte de Saint-Simon (1760-1825). Based on the necessity of creating a new society after the French Revolution which he thought had destroyed the old order, St.-Simon's ideas attempted a synthesis of religion and science, sentiment and reason. The synthesis, never too clear in his writings, did not outlast his death. Between 1825 and 1835, St.-Simonianism became a religion with a decidedly socialistic thrust. Among other things, the St.-Simonians condemned economic competition and advocated the emancipation of women. After 1832, a combination of government prosecution and divisions within the movement (chiefly over its religious extravagances) led to its collapse as a sect. Its long-term influence was felt especially, however, during the Second Empire when many ex-St.-Simonians, who had pursued the scientific and industrial interests of the original movement, contributed greatly to the economy, chiefly in the development of banks and railways. Other long-range St.-Simonian influences, significant for the problems this work investigates, can be seen in their ideas on the unity of religion and art. For a collection of St.-Simon's writings and a lucid, if highly biased, introduction,

see Henri de Saint-Simon, Social Organization, the Science of Man and Other Writings, trans. and ed. Felix Markham (New York,1964)

[6]For example, see Ruth Zabriskie Temple, The Critic's Alchemy: A Study of the Introduction of French Symbolism into England (New York, 1953), and Enid Starkie, From Gautier to Eliot: The Influence of France on English Literature 1851-1939 (London, 1960). The work by Temple contains an especially cogent discussion of the "slight spiritual community" between Baudelaire and Swinburne (pp. 99 ff.).

CHAPTER II

THE FRENCH SCENE

Desacralization in France was not a nineteenth century phenomenon. The process of secularization itself is part of the story of Western civilization; by the time of the Enlightenment, it was well advanced. The Enlightenment emphasis on reason and progress, a society responsive to laws similar to those governing the Newtonian universe (in short, a philosophy of the manageability of human affairs), administered a further blow in a centuries-long development. If human society is reducible to laws discovered through the scientific method, then indefinite man-made progress becomes a possibility. The eighteenth century is replete with such theories, of which Condorcet's is perhaps the most prominent. On the one hand, the old religious dogmas continued to exist, but without many of the societal underpinnings which had given them context and meaning; on the other, they were often adhered to even after their supporters had stopped believing. In this world of belief and nonbelief with its emphasis on human possibility, Romanticism was one response, among others, to secularization--an attempt to resacralize the world. However different Romanticism's eventual German, French, and English directions, it had vaguely religious dimensions in all these countries. Schenk and Abrams, for example, have pointed up the spiritual longings inherent in the movement--its "natural supernaturalism" and the simultaneous quest for religious belief and inability to embrace it.[1] For the Romantics, a spiritualized world still existed, but one without the parameters of revealed religion.

Because of their concern for human possibilities, both Enlightenment and Romanticism can be seen as Faustian ideas. In Goethe's Faust, when the aged and blind protagonist finally dies, only Mephistopheles imagines briefly that he has been satisfied. Angels claim Faust's soul and he is escorted into ethereal realms by young boys and his beloved Gretchen because he has striven to the end. When Goethe changed the wager in part one (from the original sixteenth-century anti-Catholic propaganda piece) so that the devil could claim Faust's soul if he could ever be satisfied, the work was read in its time as the height of Romantic literature. The never-satisfied, constantly striving Faust could not be damned for human fulfillment. But there are in Goethe's work both Romantic and Enlightenment elements. Faust desires both knowledge and sensory experience; he is simultaneously Enlightened scholar and Romantic seeker, a never-satisfied striver in either case.

By the late eighteenth century, Faustian possibilities seemed greater than ever before. Although not everyone subscribed to theories of rationality, across-the-board progress did seem to have been made in human knowledge, and it often seemed merely a matter of time before the lessons and methods of the physical sciences could be applied fully to ethics, psychology, society. Then came the French Revolution, and though the revolution appeared at first to advance the ideas of liberty, equality, and fraternity, early idealism gave way to the Reign of Terror, destruction of most Church authority in France, and exaltation of Reason to the high altar of Notre Dame. The guillotine shadowed all who questioned Reason's primacy as defined by the ruling cadres.

Half a century later, France was still in shock from the events following 1789. The degeneration of the first revolution into dictatorship, the glory of the young Napoleon dissolved into the exiled and self-pitying figure of St. Helena, the Bourbon Restoration, the July Monarchy with its greed and ill-disguised authoritarianism, and finally another Bonaparte with imperial ambitions--all this chronicles political trauma and shock. For some mid-nineteenth-century thinkers, Romanticism and Enlightenment were still sufficient areligious explanatory unities. For others, both failed, and among the most prominent of these were the "l'art pour l'art" figures. For this artistic elite, art became a response to secularization, a way of looking at the desacralized world through the prism of "l'art pour l'art." Evil could not be understood simply within the context of Romantic striving; therefore, theodicies were still needed. Enlightenment rationalism had not necessarily led to progress and could be antithetical to much in the human spirit. Theories of progress called for an antidote.

French popular and periodical literature in mid-nineteenth century reveals the similar tensions of a society desperate for meaning, often caught up in the trivial and commonplace, living an odd combination of complacency and fear. There is intense realization of living in a transitional age, of individual isolation in the new age, and the need for the creeds which became a fixture on the nineteenth-century French intellectual landscape. What is of special interest to us is the portrait of art which this literature contains (a diametrical opposition to the tenets of "l'art pour l'art"), and the implicit assumption in most of it that Enlightenment and Romanticism still have a place in France.

In most periodical literature between approximately 1830 and 1870, there is surprising continuity and agreement on art's "social function." St.-Simonian ideas on literature reflecting and leading society show an astonishing viability and diffusion. The central idea is that poetry has a moral purpose, an idea hardly original with the St.-Simonians and traceable back at least to classical Greece. But in mid-nineteenth-century France, it became a newly potent force against the background of religious disbelief and the search for secular substitutes. For the same reason, emphasis on art's "religious function" achieved a power it could not have had otherwise. Art could unite God and man, according to many of these theorists,[2] a convenient blending of St.-Simonian and socialist ideas and an equally convenient sidestepping (however unconsciously) of the fundamental religious question of desacralization.

As early as 1834, elaborate theories were worked out. In St.-Simonian thought, art seizes the living social thought (meaning the "generally dominant idea" of the moment) and reproduces it.[3] Productions of art have value only when addressed to the moral part of man and the moral education of society. For the July Monarchy, too, literary taste and morals were linked. After numerous secret societies were established in 1834, the regime took every opportunity to connect a writer's moral life with his artistic production, hoping in this way to discredit Romanticism.

Flowing from these ideas of art's moral purpose is a quasi-Romantic vision of the artist and, at the same time, a utilitarian approach reminiscent of Bentham. The artist's greatest ambition should be perfection of the moral culture; in the future, nothing can hinder perfection of thought, as political or religious intolerance conspired to do in the past. Poetry can be especially useful in drama, seen without qualification as a tool of popular education.[4] According to Comte, too, poetry when regenerated (presumably from its flirtation with Romanticism and "l'art pour l'art") can furnish a model for human conduct. The Religion of Humanity can "train the heart" through didactic art and literature.[5] At the same time, the artist is a priest who is not permitted to believe in nothingness.[6] All this rests on the fundamental idea that human nature and society are perfectible. Art's combination of the ideal with the incomplete and defective elements of reality fulfills its highest function--to aid in social perfectibility.

The ideal also compensates us for reality. In ages which are not grandiose, when reality is vulgar (mid-nineteenth-century France is the unmistakable target of these remarks), poetry is not a luxury but a passion and a survival device. Art gives human beings consciousness of themselves within their milieu,[7] but that consciousness was founded on perceptions of a future golden age based on one common interest for all humanity, progress of the sciences.[8] In a perceptive article written much later, Ernest Renan noted that St.-Simonian efforts to establish an original religion rested on a basic misunderstanding in applying the name religion to well-being and industry.[9]

These ideas on progress are worth investigating further. Though progress may have been an intellectually discredited idea by 1848 among certain elites (surely it was for the "l'art pour l'art" figures), it could not have been for society as a whole or the extant literature on progress would be neither so vast nor so encompassing in time. As late as the 1860's, the same emphasis on art for instruction's sake, scientific progress, and utilitarian and priestly conceptions of the artists' future role continue to exist. The artist alone is considered worthy to direct humanity into the future golden age because his "sympathie" allows him to embrace both God and society. Social regeneration lies in artistic regeneration.[10] In 1850, one writer claimed that the law of progress includes all prescriptions of the moral law, and that the morals of his century were generally better than those of many more ostensibly religious eras. God's own intent was the "final development of human nature,[11] presumably in some blend of artistic-moral conduct. An 1864 work, Le Progrès, returns again to the artist's role to instruct and develop specifically human sensitivities.[12] And an 1864 article in the Revue des deux mondes urges that without liberty and moral law, progress itself, "all-powerful progress," is lessened.[13] From a later perspective, Bury's 1932 work, The Idea of Progress, argues that from the Renaissance on, preconditions were set for the supplanting of Providence by Progress, and that the idea finally passed from the eighteenth century revolutionary doctrinaires to the "constructive socialists" of the nineteenth. For Bury, history itself is progress, and he connects the idea to the growth of modern society, rationalism, and the struggle for political and religious liberty.[14] Both de Liefde and Combes argue for the broad diffusion of St.-Simonian ideas throughout every level of society decades beyond the sect's dissolution in the 1830's.[15]

With these ideas of art which reduce it to the useful are similar notions of work and knowledge. The St.-Simonians saw work as adoration of the divinity.[16] This sounds very much like English periodicals of the same period, except that the English emphasis on work and progress is more pervasive, and that alongside these French reflections is a considerable body of periodical writing which did not view progress as an unalloyed blessing.

Many of these writings were specifically directed against artistic progress in the "l'art pour l'art" school; others were generalized broadsides against an increasingly incomprehensible society. Attacks against the "l'art pour l'art" advocates were based on St.-Simonian views of art expressing the state of society. The contemporary problem was considered to be "anarchy in understanding" caused by forgetfulness of tradition and absence of religious elements, both leading to exaggerated desires for happiness and the artificial.[17] Reminiscent of similar early expressions in the St.-Simonian periodical, Le Producteur, these writings maintained that the fine arts in the future would be useful, responding to majority needs and sentiments.

Beneath these outright attacks on "l'art pour l'art" were other social concerns more broadly expressed. One writer lamented the disappearance of old beliefs with nothing to replace them, but hoped with St.-Simonian direction that writers and legislators could reconcile diverse beliefs, establishing a new faith on the ruins of political and religious skepticism.[18] Another lamented the "excessive love of humanity for itself," viewing democracy as a "multiple God."[19] Another saw the era's malady in a cult of force and success, idolatry of humanity, and the chimera of happiness on earth. Intellectual life seemed no longer dominated by respect for spiritual things; the literary spirit had become a "vulgar deification of itself," and attitudes of industry reigned everywhere.[20] Human individuality seemed feeble and threatened as never before. The individual was free indeed, but on condition of isolation from his fellows.[21]

There were also a few voices pointing to the spiritual pride of the age. Writing in the Revue des deux mondes in 1850, one author praised the great achievements of the human spirit during the past three centuries through reason and liberty, but deplored the consequence that people were now convinced that nothing was henceforth impossible, that the world could be made a paradise.[22] A frequent critic of what he considered a materialistic society, Emile Montégut blamed the malaise on the false starting point of revolution. Before society could be truly reformed, the individual had to change.[23] Since the power of St.-Simonian and Fourierist doctrines lay precisely in their fusion of individual and social reform, his criticism missed its mark.

There is also in this periodical literature the familiar catalog of the literary man's vices--a class independent of all institutions, unmoved by duty, producing in the 1850's at least an imaginative literature "perhaps one of the poorest France has ever known."[24] By 1866 these social critics and adherents to St.-Simonian ideas thought poetry had all but disappeared, drowned in its own egoism, unable to endure because it did not reflect society.[25] The bourgeois wish that the novel contribute to the improvement of man and society, the glorification of virtue and flagellation of vice,[26] had gone unrealized.

What emerges from this portrait of mid-nineteenth-century France is a little different from what we might conclude from Gautier's preface to <u>Maupin</u>, for instance, or Flaubert's letters. This popular literature does not merely document contemporary views of art, among other possible reasons why an artistic elite might find its society suffocating. It also reveals a society not totally unconscious of its plight. There is a surprising, though hardly widespread, emphasis on returning to old beliefs and an intense consciousness of living in an age of transition. As we will see, the same is true of the Victorians. A further question arises of how different Baudelaire, Flaubert, and Gautier are from this climate of opinion. On the level of opposition to materialism and the cry for spiritual realities, they seem at first glance remarkably attuned to some of these periodical writers we have examined. Their differences on the subject of art, of course, are enormous and obvious. But to understand their true divergence and their historical rather than literary importance, we need to return again to the Faustian analogy.

By the mid-nineteenth century in France, the constellation of ideas was divided roughly between those for whom the popular diffusions of Enlightenment and Romanticism (elite phenomena originally) were still sufficient even after the century's catastrophes and those for whom they were not. Although many people still believed in and practiced "old fashioned" religion, our portrait of French societal and literary interests drawn from popular literature illustrates that Enlightenment views of progress and Romantic notions of the possibilities opened by human striving were far from dead. In almost infinite variety, ideas of progress and human perfectibility were still viable for many. The utopian thinkers against whom Baudelaire and Flaubert inveighed were linked both to Enlightenment rationalism and to Romanticism, a link which produced their peculiar blend of emotive fantasy and societal law. The utopians, in turn, helped extend the dialectic between Enlightenment and Romanticism far into the nineteenth century. It is arguable that even today we, too, live within the dialectical relationship of these ideas.

For most utopians, of socialist or whatever view, evil was not a permanent condition; with education and progress, it would tend to disappear. For these people, Enlightenment rationalism seemed to engender progress, usually defined as perfection of the social order, and to imply manageability. If social reality became a bit untidy at times, it was basically manageable. The spinning out of control of the late eighteenth century probably would not recur. As for the other aspect of the dialectic, Romantic striving tended to eliminate evil as surely as Enlightenment rationalism. Art's religious and social functions, examples of such striving, would eventually educate a populace able to create the perfect society.

For others, the Enlightenment and Romanticism were insufficient. We have seen this insufficiency hinted at by a few popular writers who wanted to resurrect the old beliefs or who simply cried out against too rapid and unassimilated change. What the anti-Faustian artists did was state these vague longings and focus the malaise of their age. They did indeed mirror their society, in an entirely different sense from that intended by the St.-Simonians. There is a vast difference between raising cries of moral decay (every age seems to have considered itself decadent or following the example of a mythologized version of the Roman Empire)[27] and pointing, as Baudelaire did, to the ways in which good and evil coexist. For the anti-Faustian artists, reducing the world to manageability also threatened to kill dream, illusion, recognition of limitation--all necessary to the life of the spirit. In Flaubert's eloquent term, the utopias "threatened to cover up the ruins."[28] The "ruins" were the dissolution of the centuries-old Christian ethos, the "no-man's-land" of French politics after monarchical collapse, the vulgarity of bourgeois attitudes--all the elements of the lost, desacralized world. Ideas of progress and perfectibility threatened to cover the ruins, on the one hand, by belief in human possibility, on the other, by evading the issues of limitation, sin, foolishness. This was intolerable for Baudelaire and Flaubert. Gautier, too, felt the need to deal with these issues, albeit in a re-enchanted world of dream. Even the utopians, especially Fourier and St.-Simon, wanted to rebuild the entire society.

These "ruins" are the reason why a deeper response was called for than lamenting a lost world or pointing with horror to encroaching industrialization. What Flaubert, Baudelaire, and Gautier meant at their deepest level was that Faust was dead along with everything else. Human possibilities defined from Enlightenment and Romantic positions no longer existed. The only possible response to decasralization then was an anti-Faustian posture, an artistic statement that limitation, evil, and folly exist, not merely as components of Romantic striving, and that neither rationalism nor effort can erase them or their effects. Human society is not perfectible because people are not perfectible; ultimately, there can be only the appearance of progress in technological or scientific achievement. Human beings are basically, fatally flawed. In the absence of the Christian ethic which had bound society together for centuries and explained all this, a new mythology was needed, but its creation was premature. The anti-Faust's artistic task was to point out the ruins, and to call humanity by its proper name of flawed and almost unbelievable spiritual frailty. All this and more Baudelaire and Flaubert did in their work. Even Gautier knew something of spiritual fragility.

But if the French anti-Fausts, seen as historical distinguished from strictly literary figures, search for appropriate responses to the grave cultural crisis of desacralization, their message is muted by multiple side issues to which they often seemed to give undue attention. These same issues have tended to obscure the more fundamental cultural changes of which these smaller issues were symptomatic but not inclusive.

Of the many things the "l'art pour l'art" advocates opposed, the most frequently discussed is the rise of the bourgeoisie and democracy.[29] Specifically, their opposition was directed against bourgeois vulgarity, as in Gautier's prefaces, and fears of democratic inroads into aristocratic art, which Flaubert's and Baudelaire's letters decry. Their reaction on this level was also against the advancing popular political participation with which they felt ill-equipped to deal. The "l'art pour l'art" advocates ranged themselves against post-1830 Social Romanticism, which represented basically a double message: expectation of a degree of political leadership from the nation's poets, and rewards for the more tasteless artistic productions.[30] Taste was influenced by another factor as well. Around 1830 France saw the first effects of the Industrial Revolution; henceforth there would be the means of production to provide a large reading public with a mass literature.[31] Though perhaps artists generally fared better under the rewards of the marketplace than under the patronage system of previous centuries,[32] their fulminations against politicization and tastelessness illustrate both the gravity of the cultural crisis and the difficulty in grasping it.

Many artists also opposed rationalism, socialism, and their own altered role in the world.[33] The three French anti-Fausts we will examine reacted strongly indeed against a strictly rational world and socialist schemes for utopia. As for their personal role in the world, only Flaubert seemed financially secure enough from his writings to afford the luxury of an entire book against his times like <u>Bouvard et Pécuchet</u>. Although his later years were beset with financial difficulties, they sprang from his niece Caroline's marriage, not from public lack of response to his works. The pose of the artist against society was chiefly that--a pose, like that of the dandy, valuable more for another reality to which it pointed than for itself. Certainly there was artistic uncertainty about the new society and the artist's role in it. There were the St.-Simonians, utilitarians, all the disciples of progress; the reappearance of the Bonapartist phenomenon after 1848 and cruel disappointment when the republican also became an emperor; support for a life of action valued far above intellectual effort; and finally, the artistic self-consciousness made possible since the earliest days of Romanticism.

This is a vast and familiar catalog to students of nineteenth-century intellectual history. But neither alone nor as a composite do these factors explain the deeeper cultural crisis of the nineteenth century. Nor are they merely aspects of that crisis. They are real entities in themselves, distinct problems for the nineteenth-century artist. The deeper question is how to live without the gods. Innocence and redemption, the illusion of a world set right, acceptance of sin and limitation inseparable from good--all this Christianity had explained. It still did so for many pious nineteenth-century people. For the not-so-pious, there were alternative beliefs in progress, perfectibility, or some other version of a secular religion. But the creative elite of the "l'art pour l'art" figures was seriously disoriented. These writers knew already what the twentieth century was to perceive on a broader scale, that the gods were lost or departed and man is not Faust. Their new world was basically areligious (not necessarily irreligious) and that it would remain. "L'art pour l'art" in France expressed the artistic reaction to that desacralized world and offered a limited solution.

The secular religions and utopias which flourished briefly in nineteenth-century France could hardly be expected to explain what by implication they denied. The St.-Simonians, and the followers of Fourier and Comte, staked their existence on the belief that evil could be eventually overcome. Limitation, too, was not seen as inherent in human nature, but the result of social forces which could be controlled once they were understood. To all this, the works of Baudelaire, Flaubert, and even Gautier responded with the sense of tragedy, notably missing from Enlightenment and Romantic thought. Life is tragic because evil and good are inseparable; it is short (though not necessarily nasty, brutish, solitary and poor, also, as Hobbes thought); and foolishness abounds. For the anti-Faust, there can be no progress, and reality must be assimilated anew in the face of the breakdown of the centuries-old ethos. Even in our day this new assimilation has not yet occurred. We live in fragmentation as a condition of life. Part of the message of artistic modernity is that the fragments exist of and for themselves with their own peculiar beauty. For the twentieth century, reality is a succession of discrete moments in which we all participate both as actor and observer. This is precisely the artistic stance of Baudelaire and Flaubert. For them, even desire is limited, circumscribed by personal and social forces which we can barely understand, and, ultimately, art itself cannot provide a focus for desire. What art can provide is a theodicy, a justification for human frailty and evil. We view these depths in Flaubert's characters; in Baudelaire's "flowers of evil," spleen and ideal; in Gautier's dream world.

For these three nineteenth-century literary figures, art is antidote, too. The anti-Fausts lived in a world which they often viewed as barbaric, often overwhelmed by the now-familiar grievances of the nineteenth-century artist. To this essential rootlessness, art was an antidote to belief in progress and the artist's new social role. The "l'art pour l'art" school, however diffuse and ill-named, also provided the illusory psychic strength a group gains by thrusting itself against a crude and unintelligible society. But the more important antidote was to desacralization itself. In the absence of the sacred, a sanctuary of art could be created where the fragmented world could be seen as it is--perhaps never again to be whole, perhaps permanently stripped of its gods. For French society generally, "l'art pour l'art" was insufficient, but for these three mid-nineteenth-century literary figures, it had the explanatory power of myth for the new/old phenomenon of desacralization.

Notes to Chapter II

[1]M. H. Abrams, Natural Supernaturalism (New York, 1971); H. G. Schenk, The Mind of the European Romantics (Garden City, 1969). Other works on Romanticism which are especially relevant to this point include: Albert Beguin, L'Âme romantique et le rêve (Paris, 1946), and Paul van Tieghem, Le romantisme dans la littérature européene (Paris, 1948).

[2]Victor Cousin, "Du beau et de l'art," Revue des deux mondes 2 (1845):793. For the classic statement of the St.-Simonian position on the arts, see Aux Artistes: Du passé et de l'avenir des beaux-arts (Doctrine de Saint-Simon), pamphlet (Paris, 1830), microfilm. For a good collection of St.-Simon's writings see Social Organization: The Science of Man and Other Writings, ed. Felix Markham (New York, 1964).

[3]Louis Dussieux, L'art considéré comme le symbole de l'état social (Paris, 1838), p.4; Thoré, "L'art social et progressif," L'Artiste 7 (1834): 41 f., Slatkine Reprints (Geneva, 1972); Le Producteur (Paris, 1825), microfiche, p.5.

[4]Ibid., p. 334.

[5]Auguste Comte, "The Expansion of Sympathy," from The Religion of Humanity, in French Utopias, ed. Frank E. Manuel and Fritzie P. Manuel (New York, 1971), p.347.

[6]Bignan, Essai sur l'influence morale de la poésie,p.340.

[7]Saint-René Taillandier, "Simples essais d'histoire littéraire: la littérature et les écrivains en France depuis dix ans," Revue des deux mondes 2 (1847): 981 f. Charles de Remusat, "De l'esprit littéraire sous la restauration et depuis 1830," Revue des deux mondes 2 (1847): 491.

[8]Claude Henri de Saint-Simon, "The Rule of the Scientists," from Letters from an Inhabitant of Geneva to His Contemporaries, in French Utopias, ed. Manuel, p.266.

[9]Ernest Renan, "De l'avenir religieux des sociétés modernes," <u>Revue des deux mondes</u> 5 (1860):769.

[10]Saint-René Taillandier, "La poésie et les poètes en 1865," <u>Revue des deux mondes</u> 4 (1865):617. <u>Aux Artistes: Du passé et de l'avenir des beaux-arts</u>, pp. 78, 83 f., and Barrault, <u>Le Globe</u> 7 (1831), no. 122 (no pagination), give the earlier and fuller statements of the same ideas.

[11]Auguste Javary, <u>De l'idée de progrès</u> (Paris, 1851), pp. 284, 280.

[12]Edmond About, <u>Le Progrès</u> (Paris, 1864), p. 355.

[13]Charles de Mazade, "Les idées liberales et la littérature nouvelle," <u>Revue des deux mondes</u> 2 (1864):735.

[14]J.B.Bury, <u>The Idea of Progress</u> (New York, 1932). For the references given in the text, see especially pp.234, 323, and 348.

[15]C.L.de Liefde, <u>Le saint-simonisme dans la poésie française entre 1825 et 1865</u> (Haarlem, 1927), pp. 96, 118 f., 184; Justin-Emile Combes, "Le saint-simonisme et son influence sur la littérature," <u>Revue Contemporaire</u> 46 (1865):87.

[16]Liefde, <u>Le saint-simonisme dans la poésie française entre 1825 et 1865</u>, p. 87.

[17]Émile Montégut, "Les symptomes du temps,"<u>Revue des deux mondes</u> 3 (1848): 106, 114.

[18]Hippolyte Desprez, "De la littérature et de l'enseignement populaires en France," <u>Revue des deux mondes</u> 1 (1849): 763, 786.

[19]Émile Montégut, "De la maladie morale du dix-neuvième siècle," <u>Revue des deux mondes</u> 3 (1849): 675 ff.

[20]Émile Saisset, "De l'état moral de notre époque," <u>Revue des deux mondes</u> 1 (1850): 287. For the quote on the literary spirit as a vulgar

deification of itself, see Charles de Mazade, "De la démocratie en littérature," Revue des deux mondes 1 (1850): 911.

[21]Ibid., p.1009. See also Montégut, "Simples essais sur le temps présent: De l'individualité humaine et de l'independence de l'esprit dans la société moderne,"Revue des deux mondes 5 (1856): 677 f.

[22]Saisset, "De l'état moral de notre époque, p.286.

[23]Émile Montegut, "Études morales sur la société française au XIXe siècle: La vraie cause de la crise actuelle," Revue des deux mondes 4 (1851): 202.

[24]Émile Montégut, "La littérature nouvelle: des caractères du nouveau roman," Revue des deux mondes 2 (1862): 1000.

[25]C. Martha, "La poésie du jour," Revue des deux mondes 2 (1866): 1013, 1018 f. For similar ideas elaborated a little later, see Paul Stapfer, Études sur la littérature française moderne et contemporaine (Paris, 1881), pp. 118, 133.

[26]Taine, "La poésie moderne en Angleterre," p.369.

[27]See Koenraad W. Swart, The Sense of Decadence in Nineteenth Century France (The Hague, 1964). Swart's analysis of France begins with a discussion of the fact that the idea of living in a period of political and cultural decline is as old as recorded history.

[28]Gustave Flaubert to Louis Bouilhet, 4 septembre 1850, Oeuvres complètes (Paris: Club de l'Honnête Homme, 1971-75), XIII, 76.

[29]See, for example, Albert Cassagne, La théorie de l'art pour l'art en France chez les derniers romantiques et les premiers réalistes (Paris, 1906), p. 458, and Albert Guérard, Art for Art's Sake (Boston, 1936), p.61. For a more generalized study of the artist in the nineteenth century, see Cesar

Graña, Bohemian Versus Bourgeois (New York, 1964), pp. xi, 60 f., 100, 107, and passim; and for a study of the artistic avant-garde after 1870, see Renato Poggioli, The Theory of the Avant-Garde (Cambridge, 1968).

[30]One highly perceptive critic's thoughts on bourgeois tastelessness are contained in Baudelaire's art criticism on the government-sponsored exhibitions of 1845, 1846, and 1859: Charles Baudelaire, Écrits sur l'art, 2 vols. (Paris, 1971). Re the artist's political role, see F.W.J.Hemmings, Culture and Society in France 1848-1898 (New York, 1971), pp. 8f., 150; and David Owen Evans, Social Romanticism in France 1839-1848 (Oxford, 1951), pp. 29, 37.

[31]Albert Joseph George, The Development of French Romanticism: The Impact of the Industrial Revolution on Literature (Bruges, 1955), p. 15.

[32]See Ian Watt, The Rise of the Novel (Berkeley, 1957): ". . . the booksellers actually supported more authors more generously than ever patronage had" (p. 54).

[33]For example,Graña, Bohemian Versus Bourgeois There is an especially lucid exposition of the process of rationalization as it could possibly affect the artist on page 209.

CHAPTER III

CHARLES BAUDELAIRE: ART FOR EVIL'S SAKE

Charles Baudelaire's main concern was with the perennial evil, inseparable from good, unintelligible, intractable, at the heart of human experience. Baudelaire's anti-Faustian reordering of reality first had to account for evil. Beyond that, it had to deal with the illusory, the nonobvious, spiritual face of life--all that is not progress--and in conjuring this, to re-form life.

In direct contradiction to the utopian seers of his day, Baudelaire never stopped exploring the evil that exists in the human person. After the famous address to the reader ("--Hypocrite lecteur,--mon semblable,--mon frère!"), Baudelaire's most important work, Les fleurs du mal, published in 1857, opens with the "spleen and ideal" poems. For Baudelaire, spleen is despair, melancholy, ennui from which we are rescued by and for the ideal, art. In Baudelaire's scheme of things, art becomes both the justifier of evil as the other, neglected, half of life (thus, the re-former of life) and a salvation from that evil.

Baudelaire's literary and artistic criticism explicitly develops his ideas on evil, on the human person torn between fundamental contradictions, and on all that can never be called "progress." In one of his articles on Edgar Allan Poe, Baudelaire discusses "the natural wickedness of man"--"we are all born marked for evil." In fact, the poet considers that civilized man has invented the philosophy of progress merely to console himself for his own moral abdication and decay, the immemorial reality of original sin.[1]

But not everything is spleen for Baudelaire. The conjuncture of human grandeur and misery, the simultaneous horror and ecstasy of life, a major theme in Les fleurs du mal, is ultimately a deeper realization of the human spirit.[2] Even the ability to laugh, which Baudelaire calls satanic in its revelation of human superiority over the animal world, illustrates grandeur and misery, the central human contradiction. This perception of contradiction sees human beings as fatally flawed from the beginning, with a fundamental lack running through persons and human relationships. Baudelaire's own words about original sin and the problem of evil make his position clear. Evil is indispensable to life; so is recognition of it.

> All the heresies to which I have made allusion [Fourier et al.] . . . [are] . . . above all, but the consequence of the great modern heresy, of the artificial doctrine, substituted for the natural doctrine,--I wish to say: the suppression of the idea of original sin.[3]

Baudelaire calls the peculiar malady of the eighteenth century its lack of a sense of original sin, and claims that "All literature derives from sin.--I speak very seriously."[4] In one of his projected prefaces for a new edition of Les fleurs du mal, Baudelaire speaks almost in traditional theological categories: ". . . everyone senses the devil and no one believes he is there . . . the sublime subtlety of the devil."[5] But the poet's purpose is hardly theological. As seer, he aims to extract the beauty of evil. Baudelaire asserts that evil does not need the human component, that it makes itself naturally, by fatality, without effort. The good is always the product of an art, and Baudelaire claims that most present errors in beauty are born of the eighteenth century's false conception of morality which took nature as the source and type of good and all possible beauty. On the contrary, nature produces only evil--in man, original sin and spleen, psychological evils from which we are rescued by art. But the interdependence between spleen and ideal, evil and art, is tight. They do not merely coexist; they are inseparable, mutual sources of energy. Far from being dissolved into Faustian striving, evil is for Baudelaire the indispensable other face of life which art, through re-forming nature, restores. Art as theodicy defines for Baudelaire the conjuncture of good and evil which constantly preoccupies him.

The human contradiction, its union of good and evil, is the basic reason why there can be no progress. Beyond evil and contradiction, though derivative from these, Baudelaire's reordering of the desacralized reality must deal with all the other parts of human experience not amenable to progress.

Petits poèmes en prose and Les fleurs du mal are veritable compendiums of all that is not progress. In "Le désespoir de la vieille," the poet cries, ". . . nous faisons horreur aux petits enfants que nous voulons aimer!"[6] In "Le vieux saltimbanque"[7] the old showman neither dances nor implores. Mute and immobile, he can only abdicate and renounce, like the poet degraded by misery and public ingratitude. If old age fits no scheme of progress, neither does time or death, the latter surely one of Baudelaire's constant preoccupations. The poet speaks of time's demonic cortege of remembrances and regrets, fears, anguish, nightmares, and its infinite posterity of hours, minutes, and seconds, and desires "pour tuer le temps qui a la vie si dure, et accélérer la vie que coule si lentement."[8]

Then there is the intractable quality of all experience. In "Le fou et la Vénus" the implacable Venus regards the poet's sadness and delirium with eyes of marble. "La soupe et les nuages" records the psychic distance between the cloud-watching poet and his companion who merely queries whether he has finished his soup.[9] And always there is death: "Plus encore que la Vie, la Mort nous tient souvent par des liens subtils."[10] The ties in Baudelaire's case are none too subtle. His poetry shows a fascination with death, though this is not unusual for the time. But Baudelaire's meaning is different: death is also part of life's evil face which art justifies and restores. His poetry illustrates both the range of his own interests in death and the ways in which it touches human experience. "Danse Macabre" admires Humanity's laughable contortions under every sun and climate; "Une charogne" shows preoccupation with the physical realities of decomposition; and "Les deux bonnes soeurs" paints debauchery and death as prodigal, unfulfilled, in eternal labor never bearing a child.

The poet loses his halo in the mud which facilitates his incognito plunge into the crowd, a major source of his artistic life. But the crowd is also death-producing for the poet as old saltimbanque-- or, to use Baudelaire's classic statement of the poet in "L'albatros":

> Exilé sur le sol au milieu des huées,
> Ses ailes de géant l'empêchent de marcher.[12]

Neither life nor death creates a total illusion without its other half. Like art and spleen, each completes the other. And finally all illusion of distance between reader and poet is destroyed by "Au lecteur" in which Baudelaire addresses the reader as "mon semblable,--mon frère."[13]

Old age, death, time, illusion--all these are not progress. If they are not always evil, they are, at the very least, signs of human limitation. Even at this level with Baudelaire we have journeyed far from Faust's Romantic striving in which the deed is all. Progress is impossible because human beings are imperfect, limited, even life and death inseparable.

We need not derive Baudelaire's views of progress only indirectly from the themes in his work dealing with what is not progress. Both in his imaginative works and in his letters, Baudelaire explicitly eschews nineteenth-century theories of progress. In "Le Gateau" he finds nothing more ridiculous than pretending that man is born good, and speaks elsewhere of progress and perfectibility as forms of human infatuation. In "L'essence du rire" he claims that human beings increase in evil and their knowledge of evil in direct proportion to good and their knowledge of it.[14] Some of Baudelaire's strongest denunciations of progress are in his "Exposition universelle de 1855." Baudelaire makes a long list of the faults of progress. It overshadows knowledge, swallows liberty, ignores punishment. Duty is lost, people are delivered from responsibility, disengaged from love of beauty. The infatuation with progress is a sign of visible decadence. Above all, he laments the confusion of the spiritual and material orders, the natural and the supernatural:

> Poor man is so Americanized by the industrial and "zoocratic" philosophers that he has lost the notion of the differences which characterize the phenomena of the physical

> world and of the moral world, of the natural and the supernatural.[15]

Baudelaire sees poetry and progress as antithetical forces which cannot occupy the same road, and speaks of "la grand chimère des temps modernes, le ballon-monstre de la perfectabilité et du progrès indéfinis."[16] Belief in progress is both a chimera and a form of self-conceit.

Baudelaire's letters bear out the same view of progress, though at less length: they present the identical view of forever-divided human nature and add the voice of personal pain to his anti-progress diatribes.

> . . .I kill myself, because I am useless to others--<u>and dangerous to myself</u>, I <u>kill</u> myself, because I believe myself immortal and I <u>hope</u> . . .
>
> . . .I believe that my life has been damned from the beginning, and that it will be <u>forever</u>.
>
> If ever a man has known, in his youth, spleen and hypochondria, certainly it is I. And . . . I enjoy living, . . .want to know a little security, glory, contentment with myself. Something terrible tells me: <u>never</u>, and something else tells me meanwhile: <u>try</u>.[17]

Because Baudelaire does not believe in progress, art is essential to life. In the beauty of art, Baudelaire finds an alternative world. Art provides an antidote to progress, allowing him to stand apart from his society in a magic and possible world of beauty.

Baudelaire's theory of art is inseparable from his theory of beauty. In the poet's eyes, beauty is essentially a composite of the eternal and the transitory. Each century has its own beauty, giving particularity to its art through its own passions. The nineteenth century's most salient characteristic in Baudelaire's eyes is its perpetual mourning. The artist's task is to extract from his century its particular beauty, like the painter who through color and design "makes us see and understand how we are great and poetic in our neckties and our polished boots."[18] In opposition to theories of unique and absolute beauty, Baudelaire wants to establish a rational and historical theory of beauty. He claims beauty is always dual in spite of its impression of unity: an eternal, invariable element whose quantity is difficult to determine; and a relative, circumstantial element drawn from its own epoch and style, morals, and passions. Were it not for this latter element, the former would be indigestible, impossible to appreciate, ill adapted to human nature. This duality in art is a fatal consequence of the duality in man. And this fleeting quality derived from its particular time, the transitory, the fugitive, the contingent half of art--all this is what Baudelaire means by modernity.[19]

Baudelaire sees the artist (in this case, his favorite painter, Constantine Guys) crossing the "great desert of men" to reach a more exalted end than that of the simple flâneur in the midst of the crowd: the artist searches for modernity. Suppression of this transitory element leads to the void of abstraction: each historical epoch has its own walk, its own look, its own smile, and "almost all our originality comes from the stamp that the times impresses on our sensations."[20] Such statements certainly do not read like those of a man in indiscriminate rebellion against his age. Baudelaire's sense of modernity and human frailty leads him to appreciate deeply his own century, while he never stops criticizing its blindness to evil, inattention to the erosion of time and death, infatuation with progress and perfectibility. Baudelaire's constant insistence on the historical nature of beauty is balanced by an equal attention to its bizarre quality, though even here there is a reversion to beauty's duality. "The marvelous surrounds us," the poet proclaims in his "Salon de 1846,"[21] pointing up an eternal quality in beauty. But for the true nineteenth-century artist, there is also the singular melancholy of his times. Baudelaire couples Delacroix, for example, with Dante and Shakespeare, "two other great painters of human sadness."[22]

Painting, indeed all the arts, are evocations of this marvelous though historicized world. With Gautier, Baudelaire is aware of the dream world, very close to and inseparable from the real world. As an evocation of this world, painting is almost a magic operation, but that dose of the bizarre particularizes beauty. The bizarre also makes beauty astonishing, though what merely astonishes is not always beautiful. The artist's imagination creates this new world, then assigns a place and relative value to the images and signs which express that world. In the artist's memory, objects rise "like Lazarus" and then are given "their luminous explosion in space."[23] To dream magnificently like this is not a gift given to all, but a divine and mysterious faculty by which we communicate with the dark and obscure world around us. It is one of the great privileges of art that the horrible, artistically expressed, becomes beautiful; and that "rhythmic and cadenced" sadness fills the spirit with calm joy. All lyric poetry by its very nature thus works almost fatally toward a return to a lost Eden. Everything in the lyric world--man, countrysides, palaces--becomes an apotheosis.[24]

Much of this faculty proper to the poet, in Baudelaire's opinion, has been diminished by the turbulence of material progress, and Baudelaire writes further that he is unable to understand why rational and spiritual man uses artificial means to arrive at poetic happiness, or any modern inventions for that matter (he has in mind ether and chloroform) which tend to diminish human liberty and life's indispensable sadness.[25] Baudelaire is none too clear on the latter point, however. In several letters, he refers to his own use of opium, digitalis, belladonna, and quinine.[26]

Baudelaire equates this poetic capacity to dream magnificently--imagination--with the poet's sovereign intelligence. The poet is intelligence above all because through imagination he alone is able to comprehend the universal analogy, that mystical religion called "correspondance."[27] Everything in the world is for Baudelaire a symbol. Symbolism is the language of nature which the poet not only deciphers but recreates in a totality for himself and others. The artist becomes, almost in a neo-Romantic sense, a link between man and God. Baudelaire's most famous statement of his theory of correspondances is in the poem of that name from Les fleurs du mal:

La Nature est un temple où de vivants piliers
Laissent parfoid sortir de confuses paroles;
L'homme y passe à travers des forêts de symboles
Qui l'observent avec des regards familiers.

Comme de longs échos qui de loin se confondent
Dans une ténébreuse et profonde unité
Vaste comme la nuit et comme la clarté,
Les parfums, les couleurs et les sons se repondent.

Il est des parfums frais comme des chairs d'enfants,
Doux comme les hautbois, verts comme les prairies,
--Et d'autres, corrompus, riches et triomphants,

Ayant l'expansion des choses infinies,
Comme l'ambre, le musc, le benjoin et l'encens,
Qui chantents les transports de l'esprit et des
sens.[28]

The evocation of the magic world created and ruled by imagination, the blending of sensual images in that world to the point of overripeness, the connections between spiritual and material realities, the bizarre quality of beauty--all are present in this exquisite sonnet.[29]

Baudelaire pursues an offshoot of his theory of the bizarre in the grotesque versus the comic. Baudelaire thinks laughter in general is tied to the ancient fall of man, to physical and moral degradation. One of the clearest signs of man's satanic side is the unconscious pride which laughs at others: "I do not fall; . . .my foot is firm and assured."[30] Baudelaire reasons somewhat circuitously that if the laugh is satanic it is then profoundly human, essentially contradictory, a sign both of infinite grandeur and infinite misery. But from the artistic point of view, the merely comic is always an imitation, a simple "laughing at," whereas the grotesque is a true creation, an "absolute comedy" of human elements so inextricably mixed with pre-existing things in nature that it must be understood by intuition.[31] Carried to its furthest extreme in "Une charogne," the grotesque encompasses death and decomposition in a nineteenth-century version of the medieval danse macabre. In spite of all this, Baudelaire sees the importance of frivolity in art, urging the coexistence of both the frivolous and the profound, with the serious often masked in frivolity.[32]

We have seen thus far that for Baudelaire beauty is composed of an eternal and a transitory element, that it is always bizarre in some way, and we have noted the sovereign role of imagination. Art is also for Baudelaire a remembrance of beauty implying a deformation (in actuality, a re-formation) of nature. The artist substitutes man for nature in his protest against it--a total divergence from the Aristotelean idea that "art imitates nature" which John Ruskin was reviving in England at the same time Baudelaire was expounding his contrary theory. Baudelaire argues that evil makes itself, that virtue alone is artificial (therefore, good), and that the good is always the product of an art, a "sublime deformation of nature" in an attempt to re-form it. In the human order there is no higher personification of this in Baudelaire's mind than the dandy, the artificial creation par excellence, cultivating beauty in his person, making an original in his being.[33] For himself as poet and re-former of nature, not necessarily as dandy, Baudelaire speaks elsewhere of his single, great and primary passion: "to glorify the cult of images."[34]

For these reasons, there can be no "chance" in art--and for another reason as well. The poet is the "prince incognito" very much like the dandy, who sees the world as a being at the center of that world, yet remaining hidden from it. The observer is a prince incognito, the "I" who forever tries to express the "non-I," the fleeting images of life itself.[35] If the fleeting image is to be caught, concentration and quick execution are essential, and beauty should be interpreted in simple, luminous language. Chance has nothing to do with it. Quick and concentrated execution of a work further assures that no intensity of action or idea will be lost as all the artist's spiritual strength converges toward a given point. Baudelaire quotes Emerson, "The hero is he who is immovably centered,"[36] and speaks with derision of Alfred de Musset's total inability to comprehend the work by which a dream becomes an object of art.[37] Rising from this focus on concentration, length interests Baudelaire also, almost in the degree it interested Poe in his philosophy of composition. For Baudelaire long poems are the resource of those incapable of writing short ones. All that exceeds the length of attention a human being can give to the poetic form is not a single poem. Baudelaire's concern is also with perspective. In the same letter which explains his theories of brevity, Baudelaire asks, "Have you observed that a piece of sky . . . gives a more profound idea of the infinite . . . than a grand panorama seen from the height of a mountain?"[38]

Baudelaire's concern for the single-minded creation of art seems to imply a center, inviting comparison with Roger Shattuck's views of twentieth-century art as the "still center" from which the individual perceives the world revolving around and outside him, yet indistinguishable from the self.[39] But Baudelaire is also the prince who is incognito everywhere. This seems to imply further (and so can Shattuck's words) the existence of multiple selves: if self is indistinguishable from the exterior world and that world lacks all objective order, perhaps only a fragmented self can deal with it.

Without positing a separate self for each poem, it is obvious that however much Baudelaire urges single-minded attention to the creative process, fuel for that process comes from the detached *flâneur*, an essentially multiple pose. The *flâneur* is everywhere, part of everything and nothing. But the ambivalence in this pose between involved sensibility and detachment is so strong that it is possible to wonder whether Baudelaire ever did stand apart as a *flâneur*. His poems need to be reread with this question in mind.

In *Les fleurs du mal* the poet laments time and death, damnation and love, and all the other human intersections of good and evil. In one of his projected prefaces for a new edition of *Les fleurs du mal*, Baudelaire asserts the difficulty of raising oneself toward divine insensibility.[40] But however he may have tried in his dandy pose to achieve insensibility toward the ills of his own life, some of his major themes can only be described as the height of sensibility. The poet-seer laments time as the great enemy of life and art:("--O douleur, o douleur: Le Temps mange la vie,")[41] and beauty becomes a kind of secular salvation from time and sin. The poems in explicit praise of beauty in _Les fleurs du mal_ are numerous, and the entire work should be read as Baudelaire's intent to find beauty in evil, the intersection of ugliness with beauty in that supreme deformation of nature which the poet performs and to which he points in his art criticism.

In _Petits poèmes en prose_ Baudelaire speaks of his desire to create a poetry adapted to the soul's movements, its "waves of reverie, the jolts of conscience." His medium is the crowd where the intersection of innumerable relationships gives rise to his poetic ideal--a poetry like music, but with neither rhythm nor rhyme.[42] In the crowd the poet moves incognito, as in "Perte d'auréole," precisely because he has lost his halo in the mud of the street. Baudelaire claims that "to enjoy the crowd is an art" because (having lost the halo) one must have a taste for wearing a mask. But if the poet is willing, he can find in the crowd's solitary multitudes his own salvation. There is an almost dialectical relationship between the poet's solitude and his universal communion with the unknown who pass.[43] Yet Baudelaire's sympathy for the crowd is always ambivalently merged with the dandy image. In "Chacun sa chimère" he observes the long line of passersby, each carrying his own peculiar chimera. The poet's is to be overwhelmed with indifference.[44] And his indifference is indeed a chimera. In "Les petites vieilles" Baudelaire embraces the good-evil human condition:

> Je vois s'épanouir vos passions novices;
> Sombres ou lumineux, je vis vos jours perdus;
> Mon çoeur multiplié jouit de tous vos vices!
> Mon âme resplendit de toutes vos vertus!
>
> Ruines! ma famille! Ô cerveaux congénères!
> Je vous fais chaque soir un solennel adieu!
> Où serez-vous demain, Eves octogénaires,
> Sur qui pèse la griffe effroyable de Dieu![45]

He is hardly the neutral observer either in "A une passante."

> Car j'ignore où tu fuis, tu ne sais où je vais,
> O toi qui j'eusse aimée, ô toi qui le savais![46]

For Baudelaire the shocking poet is also the redeeming poet, setting us free from false conceptions of nature, art, and self. Salvation is through immersion in beauty, in the beautiful-ugly reality which surrounds us and which the poet interprets. Seeing is the prerequisite to salvation in a world in which the poet again becomes the prophet, but of a different sort from the early Romantics. This prophet, who interprets his own time and time itself, is not at his core the detached observer. The _flâneur_'s multiple selves are protection for an almost too highly developed sensibility; the multiple projections of self protect the poet's centeredness in beauty. To be and to make beauty--to incorporate beauty within his person and to search it out even in the most unlikely places--this is the poet's task. The "still center" from which Baudelaire perceives the multiple external world is historicized, bizarre beauty; and the dandy pose, protected by the _flâneur_, is intended to personify beauty.

All this could easily add up to a theory of "art for beauty's sake." Baudelaire explicitly summarizes the poetic principle as simply the human aspiration toward a superior beauty, simultaneously independent from passion, "the drunkenness of the heart," and from truth, "the pasture of reason."[47] The generating condition, the "idée fixe," for all works of art is the exclusive love of beauty.[48]

But Baudelaire's theories of art comprise far more than a theory of "art for beauty's sake." The theories and the art itself are inseparable from the historical context of mid-nineteenth-century France. Although the poet finds his century foolish and lacking sense in everything, he thinks this is especially true of its artistic theories. His main target is the confusion between beauty and good, a point at the base of the opposition between "l'art pour l'art" and all utilitarian views of art. Baudelaire insists that the proper realm of the good is morality; of the true, science. Poetry (and sometimes the novel) should search only for beauty.[49]

Though philosophers might quarrel with Baudelaire's too-neat distinctions, his message is clear. In a letter to his mother he complains of the preoccupation with finding a moral, arguing that such narrowly defined morality is a stranger to beauty.[50] The poet thinks that every poem or object of art naturally and strongly suggests a moral, but that is the reader's affair. Baudelaire's reaction is against any exclusively moral intention in poetry. Baudelaire also resents the critic's new-found role to enter into the conscience, though the idea hardly surprises him, as he says, in an age which sees the novel as a vehicle to perfect the conscience of the masses.[51] In such an age, preoccupied with narrow considerations of morality and the usefulness of literature to advance these purposes, Baudelaire finds a horror of true art, often necessitating contrary poetic exaggerations.[52]

Yet he would have appreciated payment from that public. Despite avowals of the dandy and the *flâneur* poses, aloof from the public and claiming no need of it, Baudelaire's letters also reveal a different attitude. He writes of his pleasure in compliments on the aristocratic nature of his works, but that he wishes the crowd would pay him. It is unimportant whether his works are understood.[53] Beneath this is the poetic self who would have liked to have been understood. Baudelaire's views of the poet as albatross and old *saltimbanque* are cries of anguish.

After 1830, as we have seen, nineteenth-century French society looked for political leadership in part to its poets, then sent a double message of praise and scorn in demanding and rewarding utilitarian art. Baudelaire speaks of the adulterous, monstrous, and bizarre marriage between the literary school of 1830 and democracy.[54] Small wonder there was an artistic attraction for a bohemian counter-world. Baudelaire never managed, though, to escape his world, even in his poetry. He took that world to his poetry and transformed it there, practicing in his own art what he had theorized of poetic activity. Theory and practice are amazingly well aligned in Baudelaire. His transformed artistic world stands in direct opposition to contemporary theories of utilitarian art developed by Caro and Bignan, among others. Besides frequent references in his letters to utilitarianism, Baudelaire's literary and artistic criticism bears out a similar thesis. In a work on Poe, Baudelaire writes of "the great poetic heresy of modern times" as the idea of direct utility.[55] The idea of utility is most hostile to beauty, because beauty's object is itself. According to Baudelaire, poetry ought to descend into itself, interrogate its own soul, recall its own memories. If it follows a strictly moral end, its poetic force is diminished.[56]

True art has both utility and morality, though in an entirely different sense from that intended by the St.-Simonians or any of the other nineteenth-century visionaries against whom Baudelaire protested. Art is useful simply because it is art. To the bourgeois Baudelaire says that it might be possible to live a few days without bread, but never without poetry.[57] Art also has morality. Although Baudelaire implies this is entirely different from conventional morality, he never spells out its content. He does say that morality flows throughout poetry like the imponderable fluids in the whole machine of the world (a curious metaphor for Baudelaire to use) and that morality does not enter into poetry as a separate purpose, but mixes with it just as it mixes with life itself. The true poet is a moralist almost against his will, simply through the abundance of his own nature.[58] Baudelaire speaks of the puerile utopia of "l'art pour l'art"; in excluding morality and often even passion, it necessarily becomes sterile, a flagrant contravention of the human spirit.[59] Like Flaubert, Baudelaire considers himself a member of no specific artistic school. It is quite clear from his letters that he does not wish to be identified with any school nor to be considered the founder of one.[60] And so we have come full circle. Art has both utility and morality, both desperately needed in an age which Baudelaire considers bestial.

Although his social views are not highly developed, they support the poet's considerations of art, as might be expected. He is amused by the multiplicity of utopias of his day, but finds politics in general a science without heart, one which demands that its practitioners be both Jesuits and revolutionaries--a somewhat classic denunciation of both. Baudelaire worries about the loss of the artistocratic element in society, and even wonders if a nonaristocratic society would be a society at all.[61] This is hardly surprising from the early practitioner of dandyism who, even when his financial misfortunes no longer allowed such extravagances, never stopped thinking of the poet as the intellectual dandy, and who expressed considerable concern over the printed appearance of his works. For Baudelaire, socialism, for example, is not only inevitable but "ferocious" and "stupid."[62] He claims, at the same time, though, a horror of all the "modern rabble"--including in his denunciation academicians, liberals, virtue, vice, style, and progress.[63] The anti-bourgeois references in Baudelaire's writings, however, are surprisingly few, perhaps because his own life illustrated his feelings so clearly that there was no need to restate them. Unlike Gautier's near-ravings against the bourgeoisie in the preface to Mademoiselle de Maupin, Baudelaire's statements are more subtle. Because his views are so closely meshed with his artistic theories, it is often difficult to tell whether he is speaking facetiously or seriously when he claims not to share his brother-poets' desires to pour anathemas on the bourgeois head, and argues that the bourgeoisie should be educated to appreciate beauty.[64] That the poet has access to a privileged realm is central to Baudelaire's thought, but there is also a didactic thrust in his art criticism. It strains the imagination to think of the poet criticizing the art of his day with no other purpose than to earn a living. His critical works are too filled with expansions on his theories of beauty to deny them all instructional purposes. And unlike Flaubert, Baudelaire does not constantly lament his fate of having been born into the nineteenth century. Baudelaire's attitudes toward his century are much more ambivalent, even as he attacks Romanticism while he considers it the modern expression of beauty. Baudelaire exhibits in his poetry not merely a reaction against his century but a sympathy much like Flaubert's for the human condition.

"L'art pour l'art" itself means far more than artistic escape into a solitary world, peopled only with artistic fantasies. Art can be this, of course, but in Baudelaire's case it also explains a great deal: the existence of evil, limitation, why progress cannot be. As the anti-Faust, Baudelaire confronts evil wherever it exists. Evil would be less fascinating for him if it were not inextricably interlaced with good. There can be no clear line of separation between the good and the evil, in art or in life. For this reason, evil cannot be overcome through Faustian striving. Baudelaire's justification for evil is that neither art nor life can exist without it. Evil is original sin, the lost paradise, the other face of good, the neglected side of life. Integral to art and life, evil makes art possible. Art, in its turn, justifies evil. Human limitation can also be explained by evil's existence. Unlike the St.-Simonians and all the other utopian thinkers of his time, Baudelaire gives no credence to utopia. Art explains why progress cannot be. The perfection of society is impossible, now or ever, because people are not perfectible. Human limits impose societal limits. Baudelaire's views on evil and original sin, delineated both in his works and in his letters, also offer an antidote to nineteenth-century theories of progress which attempted to view human development as linear and inevitable. Baudelaire gives an antidote finally to desacralization.

In a "disenchanted" world, when the societal linchpin of religion at last had slipped,all kinds of secular religions began to emerge. Baudelaire never accepted any of them. Although his own views on art are too limited to comprise a full-blown secular religion, they do answer some needs traditionally served by religion. Chief among these is the perception of evil. In sharp divergence from Comte, who urged "training the heart" through didactic art and literature, and Spencer, who believed that evil was not permanent, that it would tend to disappear, Baudelaire perceives that "all literature derives from sin" and speaks of evil linked with good, fascinating to the human psyche, impossible to explain away. The imperfectible human person is limited in all ways, not the least of which is in not understanding the nature of evil. Therefore, there can be no progress and no utopia. In an inchoate version, there is much of late-nineteenth-century nihilism in these perceptions. The anti-Faust, who is simultaneously an anti-Enlightenment and anti-Romantic figure, reorders the desacralized reality by justifying evil and limitation.

Baudelaire's theodicy also justifies illusion. In the absence of religion's providing of illusions and in the insufficiencies of social utopias for Baudelaire, art fills the gap. Because there is limitation and because desire often appears to be unlimited, illusion is necessary to human existence. Through illusion the anti-Faust provides in art a focus for desire. Religion had previously provided the illusion of an eternal world, of happiness through union with God, of a world set right and redeemed. With the loss of much of society's religious component, other worlds of illusion were necessary. Perhaps the most striking example of this is Romanticism. But by the 1850's Romanticism was dead, its decline in France usually associated with the failure of Victor Hugo's Les Burgraves in 1843. For Flaubert, illusion is explored in the subjective life of his characters. For Baudelaire, illusion and limitation are objectified precisely because art re-forms life. Illusion no longer remains merely illusion. Its role is crucial in the artistic transformation of reality which the poet makes, standing at the center of his world, indistinguishable from it, yet apart from it.

In supplying art as a way to enter the world of illusion, Baudelaire as the anti-Faust also supplies satisfaction. Goethe's never-satisfied protagonist had only the poor illusion of Helen of Troy, who vanished when he first tried to clasp her. With Baudelaire, a permanent world of illusion is created, close to the Romantic dream world, close even to the macabre dream world of Théophile Gautier, but owing its primary existence to the poetic perception of evil. For Baudelaire, illusion is the intractable, the spiritual, the original, the nonobvious. Art conjures this, and in the process re-forms life, furnishing both theodicy and antidote. Baudelaire is an anti-Romantic figure because he does not believe that evil is eliminated or even understood by striving. Evil is as important to life as good. But its continued existence and the human consciousness of this make theodicies still necessary. Art becomes both a justification of evil and a salvation from it. Enlightenment rationalism, on the other hand, does not lead necessarily and inevitably to progress. Furthermore, the St.-Simonian version of progress, with its emphasis on perfectibility and manageability, threatened to kill the dream world. Baudelaire was enough of a Romantic, in the most extended sense of that term, to wish to preserve that world of illusion and focus of desire. In this broad sense, Baudelaire reaffirms the Romantic dream while remaining the arch anti-Romantic in his poetic themes and theory. He thus offers an antidote to progress as well as a theodicy.

If religion had previously provided some entree into this world of illusion, it had also provided a possibility of innocence regained through redemption. The anti-Faustian Baudelaire recaptures innocence in the alternative world of art, not precisely a dream world only, but one more whole (just as in the Christian version) because its evil half has been restored. In this sense, Baudelaire's world is a mirror image of the Christian world in which life's good face is restored through the continuing redemptive actions of Christ.

The alternative world of art, functioning both as theodicy and antidote, implies that utopia is impossible. Beyond this, it implies that utopian ideas of whatever shade are not the new religion the century seems to demand. The anti-Faust does far more than providing art as theodicy and antidote, more even than ordering reality in a disenchanted world. His reordering is in a permanently desacralized world, and one that was such for the first time. "L'art pour l'art" was a code phrase for a cultural as much as an artistic reality.

Notes to Chapter III

1Charles Baudelaire, "Notes nouvelles sur Edgar Poe," L'Art Romantique (Paris, 1968), pp. 178 f., 181. "Les Misérables par Victor Hugo," L'Art Romantique, p.380.

2For Baudelaire's views on the depth of human evil, see Mon coeur mis a nu (Paris, 1972), pp. 49, 99, 101 f.

3To Alphonse Toussenel, 21 janvier 1856, Correspondance Générale, I, 370, in L'Ouevres complètes de Charles Baudelaire, 19 vols. ed. Jacques Crépet (Paris: Editions Louis Conard, 1947). Dates given in brackets in reference to the Correspondance are those of the editor. On this point, also see Mon coeur mis a nu, p.97.

4To Poulet-Malassis, août 1860, Correspondance Générale, III, 177.

5Charles Baudelaire, "Préface," Les fleurs du mal et autres poèmes (Paris, 1964), p. 242.

6Charles Baudelaire, "Le désespoir de la vieille," Petits poèmes en prose (le spleen de Paris) (Paris, 1967), p.35.

7"Le vieux saltimbanque," ibid., p.67.

8See "La chambre double," ibid., p.43; "Les dons des fées," ibid., p.85; and "Portraits de maitresses," ibid., p. 147.

9"Le fou et la Vénus," ibid., p. 47; "La soupe et les nuages," ibid., p. 151.

10"Semper Eadem," Les fleurs du mal, p. 67.

11"Danse Macabre," ibid., p.119; "Une charogne," ibid., pp. 57 f.; "Les deux bonne soeurs," ibid., p.135.

12"L'albatros," Les fleurs du mal, p. 38. Re the lost halo, see "Perte d'auréole," Petits poèmes en prose, p.155.

[13]"Au lecteur," Les fleurs du mal, p. 34.

[14]"Le gateau," Petits poèmes en prose, p. 71. See also "Le joueur généreux," ibid., p. 112; Charles Baudelaire, "De l'essence du rire," Ecrits sur l'art, 2 vols. (Paris, 1971), I, 309.

[15]"Exposition universelle de 1855," Ecrits sur l'art, I, 380 f.

[16]"L'oeuvre et la vie d'Eugène Delacroix," Ecrits sur l'art, II, 310.

[17]To Ancelle, 30 juin 1845, Correspondance Générale, I, 71; to Mme Aupick, 4 décembre 1854, ibid., p. 317; to Mme Aupick [février ou mars 1861], Correspondance Générale, III, 263. On Baudelaire's ideas of progress, repetitive of views quoted previously, see letters to Alphonse Toussenel, 21 janvier 1856, Correspondance Générale, I., 369 f., and to Victor Hugo, 27 septembre 1859, Correspondance Générale, II, 344.

[18]"Salon de 1845," Ecrits sur l'art, I, 126.

[19]"Le peintre de la vie moderne," Ecrits sur l'art, II, 136 f., 150, 193. See also "Salon de 1846," Ecrits sur l'art, I, 253.

[20]"Le peintre de la vie moderne," Ecrits sur l'art, II, 150; the quote is on p. 153.

[21]"Salon de 1846," Ecrits sur l'art, I, 256.

[22]Ibid., p. 175.

[23]On all these points, see "Exposition universelle de 1855," Ecrits sur l'art, I, 378 f., "Salon de 1859," Ecrits sur l'art, II, 20, 27, 30, 35 f. For "their luminous explosion in space" quote, see "Le peintre de la vie moderne," Ecrits sur l'art, II, 158.

[24]"Théophile Gautier," L'art romantique, p. 255; "Theodore de Banville," ibid., p. 336. Also see the latter article for Baudelaire's theory of the union of the modern arts.

[25]Charles Baudelaire, _Les paradis artificiels_ (Paris, 1961), pp. 93, 143, 211 f.

[26]Among many examples, see the letters to Ancelle, 26 décembre 1865, _Correspondance Générale_, V, 192; to Charles Asselineau, 5 février 1866, ibid., p. 243; and to Mme Aupick, 17 février 1866, ibid., p. 269.

[27]To Alphonse Toussenel, 21 janvier 1856, _Correspondance Générale_, I, 368. On this same point, see "Théophile Gautier," _L'art romantique_, pp. 250 f.

[28]"Correspondances," _Les fleurs du mal_,Paris: Librairie Ernest Flammarion, 1964. pp. 39 f.

[29]Leo Bersani has suggested a fresh interpretation for the blending of sensual images in "Correspondances": "The overpowering sensation, merely by virtue of its strength, propels us out of sensation; it spiritualizes itself by its very intensity. This appears to be one of the more neglected meanings of 'Correspondances.'" Leo Bersani, _Baudelaire and Freud_ (Berkeley, 1977), p. 32. Bersani argues that certain stimulants carry the senses beyond themselves; and that viewed from their effect on the senses, these stimulants are "infinite things." One can agree wholeheartedly with this fairly evident psychological truth without necessarily accepting Bersani's conclusion that "sensuality spiritualizes" (p. 33). That "the sensual" in some way and under some conditions spiritualizes may be closer to what Baudelaire intended.

[30]"De l'essence du rire," _Ecrits sur l'art_, I, 306.

[31]Ibid., pp. 307, 312 f.

[32]To Felicien Rops, [21 février 1866; date given in footnote, letter undated], _Correspondance Générale_, V, 289.

[33]_Re_ Baudelaire's theories on the de-formation and re-formation of nature, see "Salon de 1846," _Ecrits sur l'art_, I, 224; "Le peintre de la vie moderne," _Ecrits sur l'art_, II, 180 f., 183. On the dandy, see "Le peintre de la vie moderne," pp. 172 ff.

[34]*Mon coeur mis a nu*, p. 127.

[35]"Le peintre de la vie moderne," *Ecrits sur l'art*, II, 146. See also "De l'essence du rire," *Ecrits sur l'art*, I, 324, *re* the human power to be simultaneously self and other.

[36]"L'oeuvre et la vie d'Eugène Delacroix," *Ecrits sur l'art*, II, 303. For Baudelaire's theories on the execution of art, see also "Salon de 1846," *Ecrits sur l'art*, I, 200.

[37]To Armand Fraisse, 18 février 1860, *Correspondance Générale*, III, 38.

[38]Ibid., 19 février 1860, pp. 39 f.

[39]Roger Shattuck, *The Banquet Years: The Origins of the Avant Garde in France: 1885 to World War I* (New York, 1968), p. 352.

[40]"Préface des Fleurs," *Les fleurs du mal*, p. 244.

[41]"L'ennemi," *Les fleurs du mal*, p. 44.

[42]"A Arsène Houssaye," dedication of *Petits poèmes en prose*, pp. 31 f.

[43]"Les foules," *Petits poèmes en prose*, pp. 61 f.

[44]"Chacun sa chimère," *Petits poèmes en prose*, p. 46.

[45]"Les petites vieilles," *Les fleurs du mal*, pp. 110 ff.

[46]"A une passante," *Les fleurs du mal*, p. 114.

[47]"Notes nouvelles sur Edgar Poe," *L'art romantique*, p. 189.

[48]"Théophile Gautier," *L'art romantique*, p. 245.

[49]To Alphonse Calonne, 8 janvier 1859, *Correspondance Générale*, II, 255.

[50]To Mme Aupick, 3 avril 1861, Correspondance Générale, III, 269 f.

[51]Re this point, see Baudelaire's letter to A. C. Swinburne, 10 octobre 1863, Correspondance Générale, IV, 198. Also see the letter to Jules Barbey d'Aurevilly, [9 juillet 1860? postmark illegible], Correspondance Générale, III, 137.

[52]To Victor Hugo, 27 septembre 1859, Correspondance Générale, II, 344. See also the letter to Ancelle, 18 février 1866, Correspondance Générale, V, 279.

[53]To Poulet-Malassis, 14 juillet 1860, Correspondance Générale, III, 148.

[54]"Anniversaire de la naissance de Shakespeare," L'art romantique, p. 406.

[55]"Edgar Allan Poe, sa vie et ses ouvrages," L'art romantique, p. 124.

[56]"Notes nouvelles sur Edgar Poe," L'art romantique, pp. 183, 188.

[57]"Salon de 1846," Ecrits sur l'art, I, 139.

[58]"Les drames et les romans honnêtes," L'art romantique, p. 86; also see "Salon de 1846," Ecrits sur l'art, I, 139 ff., and "Victor Hugo," L'art romantique, p. 310, for the metaphor.

[59]"Pierre Dupont," L'art romantique, p. 73.

[60]To Ancelle, 18 février 1866, Correspondance Générale, V, 281; to Mme Aupick, 5 mars 1866, ibid., p. 302.

[61]To Felix Nadar, 16 mai 1859, Correspondance Générale, II, 320 (re politics without heart). See also Mon coeur mis a nu, p. 63. To Alphonse Toussenel, 21 janvier 1856, Correspondance Générale, I, 369, re loss of the aristocratic element in society.

[62]To Ancelle, [décembre] 1849, Correspondance Générale, I, 114.

[63]To Ancelle, 18 février 1866, Correspondance Générale, V, 281.

[64]See the opening pages of "Salon de 1845" and "Salon de 1846," Ecrits sur l'art, I, 53 ff. and 139 ff.

CHAPTER IV

GUSTAVE FLAUBERT, THE ARTIST AS ANTI-FAUST

For Gustave Flaubert the human heart is perverse and foolish beyond all imagining. His novels create classic worlds of the human heart--Emma Bovary's pathos; the strange and moving portrait of St. Antoine's spiritual state; Felicité, who confuses her beloved parrot with the Holy Spirit. Flaubert once wrote that Shakespeare had worlds within him. The phrase is equally descriptive of the nineteenth-century French novelist.

Flaubert's characters live in worlds of evil, foolishness, limitation, societal damage to the individual, and illusions larger than reality while both remain hopelessly small. To enter Flaubert's world is to enter these many worlds. In all of them, evil, foolishness and illusion require the theodicy which art furnishes. As a type of the anti-Faust, Flaubert opposes Romanticism in his artistic theories. But he is anti-Romantic in a more profound sense. Flaubert's is a pessimism (unlike the more generalized "mal du siècle," a possible component of Romanticism) which rises directly from the perception that the follies and evils of the human heart cannot be eradicated by striving. And he reacts as strongly as Baudelaire against Enlightenment rationalism's legacy, theories of progress. His antidote, like Baudelaire's, is art. In the desacralized nineteenth century, Flaubert's anti-Faustian reordering is both theodicy and antidote, his worlds both illusion and reality.

Another of these worlds, not so obvious perhaps as provincial Rouen or fourth-century B. C. Carthage, is the world of his letters. Flaubert wrote thousands of letters during his lifetime, and they are among the jewels of nineteenth-century French literature. They range from discussion of art with his one-time lover, Louise Colet, to the many notes signed "Polycarpe" after the early Christian saint who constantly lamented his sad fate of having to live in the second century. There are travel letters from his Near Eastern journey, as fascinating as Gautier's travel literature; amusing letters which hold his verve and wit; glimpses of the artist at work for years on each of his "beloved old books," and much that is a portrait of his age.

Flaubert's reactions against his society are not merely in a generalized, anti-bourgeois sense.[1] His letters reveal his specific opposition to socialism, to utopias of all sorts ("all those deplorable utopias which agitate our society and threaten to cover up the ruins"),[2] and to the "man of action" ideal created by half a century of revolution in France. Like many nineteenth-century figures, Flaubert is painfully conscious of living in a transitional era, a time simultaneously too early and too late. In his eyes the times are sad--tormented by the future, held by the past.[3] Perhaps Baudelaire expresses more eloquently the "perpetual mourning" of the nineteenth century, but Flaubert's letters capture its flavor with equal accuracy.

Above all, he abhors concentration on utopian ideals. Even after the debacle of 1848 made utopianism less attractive, it remained one of his intellectual targets throughout his life. For Flaubert, utopianism inevitably leads to the "adoration of humanity for itself," a Pandora's box of ills.[4] In Flaubert's view of the socialist ideal, for example, the state becomes a vast monster, absorbing all personality and thought. At the base of the socialist structure, he sees a "sacerdotal tyranny."[5] The novelist thinks that "narrow-hearted" people have become more fanatical than ever, fears universal suffrage, and opposes equality because it seems to mean negation of liberty. Reduction to a "common mediocrity" implies that social equality has passed to spiritual equality, resulting in a conspiracy against both poetry and liberty.[6] Only art remains as the realm of freedom.

Flaubert has another reason for objecting so vehemently to the socialists. Like Baudelaire, he is disturbed by the increasing encroachments of materialism to the detriment of the spirit. Flaubert wrote to Turgenev that never had spiritual interests counted less, and that he was not disturbed so much by the political state of France, even in 1872, as by its mental state.[7] With Baudelaire, Flaubert thought all his life that the socialists denied sadness; but unlike the poet, he also thought that the socialists denied "the blood of Christ flowing in us"[8] --a highly un-Baudelairean statement and one rather surprising in the anticlerical Flaubert. His distinction between creeds and the religious spirit illuminates his initially puzzling comment. Flaubert has no use for dogmas, but states flatly that people cannot live without religion.[9] More sympathetic toward religion than Baudelaire, he is merely anticlerical, not anti-religious.

The adoration of humanity for itself, of which Flaubert accuses the socialists, will be unmasked only when people realize that "love of humanity is as shabby as love of God has become."[10] This fascination with human betterment has a positive aspect, however, in what Flaubert calls the "anatomy of the human heart." He thought his century's unique glory would be to have begun these studies.[11] His own novels certainly did so, though hardly in the cruel and crude way the famous "Punch" cartoon showed of Flaubert dissecting Emma Bovary with her heart pinioned on the end of his knife.[12] In Flaubert's opinion, his century's desire "to ascend to the sky" called first for enlargement of the human spirit. At the base of all social utopias he finds tyranny and death for the soul.[13]

For these reasons, and because the masses will always exist, Flaubert thinks that in every age a small group has been conscious of its world. In his own age, when the foolishness of the bourgeois and the country as a whole are united, the "emmerdement" is complete.[14] The earth is limited, but human foolishness infinite: hence the necessity of living in an ivory tower. Toward the end of his life, Flaubert thought that the theory of evolution had rendered a strange kind of backhanded service to French society--applied to history, it had negated all social dreams. He observed that among the socialists only "the fossil Louis Blanc" remained.[15]

But in the world in which Flaubert spent most of his life, socialism was a highly visible ideal. In such a world, which he considered savage and ugly, Flaubert thought that humanity as a whole was like a tribe lost in the desert, adoring idols. Many of his compatriots seemed to search in the flesh, others in old religions, others in art; thought alone remains eternal.[16] The converse of this is Flaubert's disgust with action as the animal side of existence. In Flaubert's world, there is no question of the primacy of intellectuals over activists. For the man of spirit, art functions to conjure away the burden and bitterness of human life. "La vie humaine est une triste boutique,"[17] the novelist concludes, and says elsewhere that beauty is incompatible with modern life.[18] Unlike Gautier, who was able to see something beautiful in the coming industrial age even while he lamented its ugliness, or Baudelaire, who searched for the specific beauty of his own age, Flaubert thought that the more a work represents humanity at all times, the more beautiful it is.

In his own utilitarian, materialistic, hideous world, Flaubert thinks that the mandarin like himself no longer has a place,[19] and expresses astonishment at all a person can suffer without dying. Although he felt this way all his life, the feeling was especially keen at the 1871 fall of Paris when Flaubert likened his own reaction to that of Rachel weeping for her lost children.[20] But Flaubert was hardly the patriot this could imply. He considered the public and the government the two greatest enemies of writers, the public because literary style forces it to think and the government because literary power competes against its own power. Flaubert could speak of weeping like Rachel because the pessimistic writer had another side. He writes that we can never have enough of human sympathy and that he does not love literature best of all:"Je ne suis pas si cuistre que de préférer des phrases à des êtres."[21] Perhaps Polycarpe was never really bitter.

Much of this supposed bitterness is not directed only against the socialistic and utopian dreams of his age, but also against organized religion. Flaubert thinks that superstition, as an eternal sentiment of the soul, lies at the base of all religion and explains that by superstition he means an unchanging belief in a force superior to life and the need for its protection. He views dogma as a purely human affair, concluding that religion thus defined is a human invention. The fanaticism of the superstitious religious sentiment itself, Flaubert compares to the artistic sentiment, eschewing fanaticism only in a narrow-minded, dogmatic sense. Art and Religion remain for him two great manifestations of idea, and the sentiment which engenders religion the most natural and poetic of humanity. Flaubert is obviously attracted by this generalized religious sentiment, repulsed by dogma; and he states so explicitly.[22] The religious and artistic sentiments are part of an immense hunger for the infinite in which the soul makes dreams, verse, melodies, ecstasy. In short, the soul makes art, and the process is complete when art in its turn makes us dream.[23] Art creates an alternative world.

In this alternative world which his letters capture as well as his novels (through Flaubert's study of the human heart), art creates a theodicy to justify evil, sadness, limitation, folly. In Flaubert's novels, evil and limitation are as necessary as good. These are not merely accepted as parts of human life over which his characters have little or no control, but vindicated as fundamentally and rightfully belonging to human existence. There was a necessity for this kind of justification because the utopians of Flaubert's day had denied evil and limitation their inevitable role. Flaubert's theodicy specifically gives limitation and illusion, quasi-evils in themselves, their right to exist as the truly indispensable side of human life. Because his characters (with a single exception) do not grow, his novels can be read as one long brief against the theory of human perfectibility. Flaubert's works are also an antidote because they reorder the desacralized reality in the magic/religious world of art, creating another world above the natural one in which the ideal consoles us for reality.[24] The artistic theories underlying these works are contained in Flaubert's voluminous correspondence, and all support this thesis of an alternative world functioning as antidote and theodicy.

Flaubert's ideas of art revolve around the possibility of making art for itself alone, a central reason why even in his own time he was often viewed (for example, by Walter Pater) as a major spokesman for "l'art pour l'art," though, like Baudelaire,

Flaubert himself eschewed belonging to any school, realist or otherwise. What Flaubert meant, though, by making art for itself alone is more complex than it appears at first. In his letters Flaubert urges that impersonality in art is the sign of strength. By impersonality, Flaubert wants the artist to "absorb the object"[25]--a direct contravention of much in Romanticism. Flaubert's denunciations of sentiment are frequent and stinging. External reality must enter into us, "making us almost cry to reproduce it well." For this reason, Flaubert thinks that the less one senses a thing, the more likely one is to express it as it is.[26] His is not an ideal in any absolute sense, but, as Flaubert himself explains about Salammbô, an ideal recreation of fourth-century B. C. Carthage as it can be reconstructed from a nineteenth-century viewpoint.[27] Whatever realism meant to Gustave Flaubert (and he sometimes does mean a dissection of life),[28] he had no question in his historical works but of a dialectic between his own century and the reconstructed period. In these works it is easy to see his claim that illusion is the first quality and purpose of art,[29] that even Madame Bovary was a complete fabrication, having no basis whatever in reality.

Flaubert's worlds of illusion range from Salammbô and L'éducation sentimentale to the trials of the desert hermit Saint Antoine, to Felicité's parrot/ Spirit complex in Un coeur simple; and he thinks that illusion is inseparable from the creation of beauty. Flaubert argues that, just as poetry transfigures objects without changing them, the most beautiful works are the least material. He once wondered if it would be possible to write a book about nothing, almost without a subject.[30] He came closest to this in Bouvard et Pécuchet, but whereas his characters are scantily drawn in that novel, its subject has been variously interpreted as the encyclopedic ills to which Flaubert thought the nineteenth century was prone, the folly of human thought itself, the egotism and arrogance of all mankind. Rather than stating a possible artistic ideal, a book without a subject, Flaubert's words underline his views of the impersonal artist. He often states that the author in his work should be like God in the universe--present everywhere, visible nowhere.[31] Flaubert returns frequently to the notion that nothing is weaker in art than the expression of personal sentiment. We have come round again to his idea of the object as the True, and the only way to great emotional effects. One starts with the external reality, not with an internal state. The individual artist is nothing, the work of art everything. By Flaubert's own admission, this is a hard discipline to observe, one requiring a permanent sacrifice to good taste. Technical detail likewise is secondary in the author's search above all for beauty.[32] This is highly reminiscent of Baudelaire's theories of art, though Flaubert's beauty is more idealized. But like the poet, he stresses that a writer must describe the milieu he knows.[33] In art everything depends on the conception:"an image . . . clear in the head leads the words onto the paper."[34]

Much of this in Flaubert's letters reads like overstated Platonism. What is crucial to remember is that most of these letters on art were written to Louise Colet, who had a decided penchant for sentimental poetry. Flaubert's urgings toward impersonality are almost always intended as correctives to her poetic stance. Though he disliked the expression of personal emotions and urged that art be seen as its own object, Flaubert is far indeed from denying subjectivity in art. Basically, his views on subject and object in art are similar to Baudelaire's. Both writers see the artist at the center of his world, distilling reality into his works. The distillation is an artistic version of reality.

When he wrote his novels, Flaubert was extremely conscious of his own role. He sees talent above all in choice of words--precision makes strength, just as in music purity of tone is essential above all else. In another image, he considers that the phrases in a book should be like leaves in a forest, each moving differently yet resembling each other.[35] For Flaubert, style is integral to thought. In one letter he describes style as the lifeblood of thought. The total creation should be a perfect linking of thought with form, because there can be no beautiful thoughts without beautiful forms. Over and over, Flaubert insists that the idea does not exist except through the form.[36] Again, all this is not so Platonic as it sounds, certainly not in Flaubert's novels; even in his letters he stresses the subject-object relationship. He is aware, for example, that memory idealizes and thinks that the eye probably does also. A photograph is never precisely what one has seen, and extending this line of thought, artistic intuition almost comes to resemble hypnotic hallucination. When the object enters into the artist, there is an interpenetration in which the personality almost escapes. The images which arise from the artist are like waves of his own blood. Like a good mime seeing and being penetrated with persons, the artist opens himself to the terror of artistic/hypnotic hallucination. Flaubert traces the process for himself. First there is indeterminate anguish, a vague malaise, as the writer arrives at poetic inspiration. Then comes the sudden eruption of memory, because the hallucination (for Flaubert, at least) comes from his memory--a statement which raises fascinating questions about Saint Antoine's hallucinations. The lone image grows until it covers all objective reality. The artist fears thinking about anything different at this point, knowing simultaneously that the thing is basically an illusion but perceived with all the clarity of reality. In sleep there is a similar state. When one knows that he dreams, everything becomes dream.[37]

Baudelaire's views of all this are somewhat different. Although, like Flaubert, he sees the artist at the center of his world, apart from it and yet indistinguishable from it, he never seems to fear personality loss in artistic hallucination. In fact, this is precisely his argument against drugs in _Les paradis artificiels_--that they provide a false path to poetic inspiration and risk personality dispersion. Whether this was a consistent fear for Flaubert, we will probably never know. Though not a consistent theme in his letters, Flaubert's concern for personality loss does show some fear which may have been inevitable for him in the artistic process.

Flaubert is closer to Baudelaire in his enjoyment of corruption in things considered pure. He searches for vileness beneath beautiful appearances, and for virtue beneath ignoble surfaces.[38] Perhaps the most striking illustration of this in Flaubert's works is the beggar figure from La légende de saint Julien l'Hospitalier. Although we will examine the story later in detail, it seems important to note here that the orgasmic ecstasy Julien experiences with the beggar occurs only because he is willing to let the vile creature into his bed. In Salammbô, likewise, the ugly and beautiful coexist. Some scenes of carnage in that novel almost strain violence to its limits. And there is very much in La tentation de saint Antoine that allies the ugly with the beautiful in Baudelaire's fashion. Flaubert's purpose, though, at least as stated in his letters, is somewhat different from Baudelaire's. Whereas the poet sought to comprehend the intersection of good and evil in human existence, the novelist claims his interest is to laugh at the human experience. Beneath everything he finds vanity, and exposes it by discovering hidden corruption. This is as close as Flaubert comes in the explication of his artistic theories to denouncing social hypocrisy, though he attacks it explicitly in Madame Bovary, L'éducation sentimentale, and Bouvard et Pécuchet.

Flaubert's views on the artist in society likewise are unwavering and these are constantly expressed in his letters. In a savage age it is necessary "to make an egoism" and live there "loving art as the mystics love God."[39] Flaubert thinks that sometimes his hatred for the public approaches Marie Antoinette's. He describes the bourgeois as a man of half-character, half-passion; a man of action and limited sense. The artist can survive only in his ivory tower, alone in his dreams like a Bedouin in the desert.[40] (Flaubert had some experience of the desert through his Middle Eastern travels, so the image was real to him.) If one truly loves literature he will make it for himself alone. Flaubert's views on the bourgeoisie are closer to Gautier's than to Baudelaire's, though all three used this class as a foil for their opposition to utility in art. Whether utility and narrow moralism were necessary components of the mid-nineteenth-century French bourgeois outlook is another matter. The point is that these three writers thought they were. Flaubert offers more diatribes against utilitarian art even than Gautier, but whereas Gautier flatly opposes the beautiful to the useful, Flaubert's explicit anti-bourgeois concern is with morality in art.

Like Baudelaire, Flaubert thinks that narrowly moral preoccupations ruin imaginative works. Like Swinburne, he rants against the "profoundly stupid thing" of making art accessible to children.[41] But for Flaubert true art is profoundly moral, consisting in beauty alone. He compares the artistic ideal with the sun's relationship to everything else--everything becomes beautiful and moral. If the reader cannot pull out the morality of a book, Flaubert sees two possibilities: either the reader is an imbecile or the book is false. Truth is good, and obscene books are simply those which lack truth. As for literature's supposed obscene tendencies, he observes that with this theory of tendencies one could guillotine a sheep for dreaming of being a bull.[42]

In spite of these Baudelairean sentiments about morality in art, Flaubert is closer to Gautier in believing throughout his life that science and art can be mutually supportive.[43] He stands midway between Baudelaire and Gautier in his perceptions of his own century. He does not join Gautier in applauding the railroad or in defining art as the "science of charm and beauty." Nor does Flaubert agree with Baudelaire that photography is inimical to true art (though he disliked photography). In the coming scientific/artistic age, art will be more necessary than ever. "Les arts et le commerce" opposes art to commerce, though stops short of condemning the latter. Flaubert is content to explain commerce as the dispenser of riches, but art remains the soul's highest manifestation. He speaks of immense hunger for the infinite, and queries that if a person does not sense this in himself, what right has he to speak of intelligence and thought.[44] In highlighting the differences among Baudelaire and Gautier and Flaubert in their stance toward their century, it must be underlined that all three were basically in agreement. Art was a citadel in a savage world, a kind of religious retreat.[45]

Art had another quasi-religious dimension for Flaubert, nowhere more strikingly displayed than in the stray dog episode from La première éducation sentimentale. Although the work is highly lyrical in comparison with the later novels and filled with awkward stylistic interruptions, there are fascinating glimpses of the mature author. For Flaubert's views on art, the central incident (more central than any other single incident in his novels) is that of the stray dog. Jules, one of the boyhood friends around whom the story revolves, cannot get rid of the animal which follows him everywhere. When he thinks he has finally banished it, he finds the creature lying on his threshold. What makes the incident significant is that there is no question Jules has dreamed this. Fear, fascination, terror, and tenderness operate in the young man's perceptions of the dog. The experience is variously described as sinister, seductive, intimate, clear, and culminating in a different kind of reality.[46] Perhaps art is the pursuing monster which is all these things. Or perhaps the creative process ranges from sinister to clear perception of new reality. Flaubert's letters certainly support such an interpretation. It is also possible from this to see Flaubert's alternative world of art as a quasi-religious world in Rudolf Otto's sense of the "mysterium tremendum."[47] Art (like the experience of God) is overwhelming, fearful, fascinating.

Art also offers a totally areligious explanation for limitation, evil and folly. As the anti-Faust, Flaubert explores worlds in which neither rationality nor human striving prevail. He ushers us into the lives of protagonists who are, in Victor Brombert's phrase, "heroes and victims of a limitless quest,"[48] but whose realities are circumscribed by limitation and whose grappling with the dark and intractable side of life is almost invariably based on illusion.

If there is one major theme in Flaubert's novels, it is illusion. Differently expressed, human beings are not Faust. Even their illusions are smaller, intertwined with reality. In none of Flaubert's novelistic worlds is there progress. To enter these worlds is to see illusion running close to life's core, but hidden from the protagonists. Evil and limitation are neither eliminated nor understood by striving, and rationalism does not lead necessarily to progress. Though Bouvard et Pécuchet is a broadside against progress, there is an anti-progress, anti-rationalism bias in all Flaubert's novels. His alternative worlds deal specifically with limitation, foolishness, illusion, sin--all the human failings which religion had previously explained. The artistic act of creating an alternative world implies a kind of escapism, the antidotal side of Flaubert's posture and part of the "l'art pour l'art" tradition itself. But the quasi-evils of limitation and illusion ultimately can be neither escaped nor precisely redeemed. They are the indispensable dark parts of life which explain why experience is fundamentally unassimilated for Flaubert.

In Madame Bovary, Emma's limitations never completely dissolve into her illusions. She is neither an evil nor a totally foolish figure. But limited she is. When both lovers desert her (when her illusions die), she too must die. If ever a figure could be called "striving," it is Emma Bovary. Yet the striving doubles back on itself, leading nowhere. Her limitations cannot be bridged or eliminated by striving. Just as Emma's involvements with Rudolf and Leon do not translate into the romantic world of the novels she reads, Charles Bovary remains the limited, ineffectual provincial doctor. The general mood of the novel is one of suffocating limitation. Even Emma's desires are limited by what she has read and the two lovers she has known. As for progress, there is none. If Emma had not died, it is hard to imagine her changing. And the characters of Charles and Homais are as viciously drawn as anything in Flaubert's works. The bungling physician and the all-knowing pharmacist carry a partial message of what Flaubert thinks of these real-life types, both much more important since the Enlightenment. These supposedly rational men are mercilessly caricatured. Granted that Flaubert had intensely personal reasons for disliking the medical profession, he shows greater sympathy for almost any of his other creations than for either Charles or Homais.

The same perception of limitation and lack of progress is applicable to L'éducation sentimentale and Salammbô. The novels are an interesting pair, in that the former deals with Flaubert's age, the generation immediately preceding his own, the latter with fourth century B. C. Carthage, but as we have seen, through a nineteenth-century prism. L'éducation sentimentale, like Madame Bovary, can be read as a novel of limitation, enclosure, stasis. Frédéric learns something of worldly ways, of life and illusion, through his experiences, but it is hard to imagine any substantial change in Frédéric as in Emma Bovary. However else the magnificent last scene between Frédéric and Madame Arnoux has been interpreted, it also says much about Flaubert's views on limitation and lack of progress. Frédéric's ideal love has aged; she remains finally and irrevocably unnattainable for reasons that would have shocked a younger Frédéric. Yet this older, only slightly wiser man is torn between repulsion and an almost incestuous interest in this mother figure before him. When she leaves, he watches her from the window. And that is all. Both characters are limited by their mutual perceptions, by time, by what they are and have been. The same is true when Frédéric and Deslauriers revisit the brothel in the novel's very last scene. Here too limitation and illusion exist on many levels: Frédéric's speechlessness upon presenting his flowers to the laughing women, his embarrassment which forces Deslauriers also to leave since Frédéric has the money, and finally their mutually agreed-upon remembrance of the brothel as having provided their best times. The fusion of past illusion in the memory with present illusion is complete. These figures are also anti-progress types, "enlightened," vapid, flawed. It is crucial in this connection to remember that the novel deals with the revolution of 1848, and its characters, more than any of Flaubert's other novelistic creations, are perhaps ones for whom the author had personal models.

In the case of Salammbô, at first reading, nothing seems drawn from life. The setting of fourth-century B. C. Carthage and the strange other-worldly quality of the protagonists make this an entirely different kind of novel. It is closer to La tentation de Saint Antoine than any of Flaubert's other works, though the author's enjoyment in describing sumptuous feasting anticipates Hérodias. In Salammbô he also seems to enjoy describing incursions of the gods, in this case the sun and moon, into human life. Mâtho and Salammbô are god-foils for each other, as well as love-foils. But their illusions of happiness together are dashed by their society, and both must die as surely as Emma Bovary. Limitation plays on many levels in this novel. There is the obvious impossibility of Mâtho's and Salammbô's love; the barbarism of war leading to dubious conquests; the inevitability of Mâtho's death at the crowd's hands. There is neither progress nor rationality. In fact, the novel deals with the irrational far more than any of Flaubert's other works, with the possible exception of <u>Saint Antoine</u>. In <u>Salammbô</u>, the irrational is outside the protagonists in the form of slaughter, carnage, and cannibalism. We need not go far to illustrate the novel's anti-rational, anti-progress intent. But in <u>Saint Antoine</u> the irrational is interior, not carefully delineated as such, ambiguous--making the work much more important for our present purposes.

The story is structured around the temptations of the desert saint, and Flaubert thought about it and worked on it intermittently throughout most of his life. The "preliminary temptations" include the Queen of Sheba and the seven capital sins. With the help of Hilarion, who eventually reveals himself as Satan, Antoine sees a procession of all the pagan gods created and used by mankind but who are now unimportant. Then he journeys to the stars. When he has seen fabulous people and beasts, the hermit exclaims deliriously:

> 'O bonheur, bonheur! J'ai vu naître la vie, j'ai vu le mouvement commencer . . . je voudrais avoir des ailes . . . pénétrer chaque atome, descendre jusqu'au fond de la matière,--être la matière!'[49]

The novel can be seen as a psychological drama or as a tour de force in demonology and mythology; and this famous ending has been interpreted variously as to whether in fact Antoine did resist temptation. But that is not the point. In his dreams, visions, temptations, the hermit experiences all the world--the material world and even something of the spiritual. His trip to the stars is literally a Faustian excursion. In the end he tries to have both God and the world. He has neither, making irrelevant the question of whether or not he resisted temptation. Flaubert may have been saying something about the religious mentality (which we will explore more thoroughly in his Trois contes), but certainly this is also a novel of limitation and anti-progress irrationality. Mythologies throughout the centuries dissolve into Antoine's experience and everything becomes essentially and finally irrational. Limitation is expressed best in the last scene. After everything, Antoine wishes union with matter. His striving leads neither to surmounting temptation nor to eliminating or understanding evil. He remains torn between God and world, possessing neither--another of Flaubert's trapped, irrevocably flawed and limited characters.

Flaubert's Trois contes deals with the same themes, though with an even more specifically religious thrust. Religion is central to the characters' experiences in all three stories. Beyond this Flaubert may have intended a comment on religious experience of his day, perhaps of Western Christendom in general. The three stories view religion variously: as an embalmed carcass, as orgasmic ecstasy, and as a consuming courtesan. The first, Un coeur simple, portrays a maidservant who deeply cherishes her pet parrot. In her spiritual and psychological simplicity, she confuses the bird with the Holy Spirit depicted in the stained glass windows of her local church. The confusion lasts. As Félicité is dying, she imagines the Spirit/parrot coming for her soul. Her life-sustaining myth thus becomes death-encompassing. Dream and reality are hopelessly mixed. Like the embalmed carcass of the parrot, Flaubert seems to say that formal religion too is kept around because human beings cannot live without it. But this is far indeed from Flaubert's meaning in his letters when he speaks of the impossibility of living without religion, an eternal, natural, and poetic sentiment of the soul. In the story the parrot carcass defines belief and is essentially irrational. Again the ending leads nowhere, though Flaubert is more sympathetic to Félicité than to most of his other characters.

In La légende de saint Julien l'Hospitalier, Flaubert paints religion as orgasmic ecstasy for the believer. Oddly enough, this is the one story in which any character of Flaubert's is saved, even in a secular sense. Julien is redeemed through suffering and service. There is considerable ambiguity in the story: the animals hating and loving, being hated and being loved; the rehearsed murder and the real murder of Julien's parents. But there is no ambiguity about the ending. When Julien allows the filthy leper to share his bed, he finds Christ. In every one of Flaubert's novels except this, there is limitation and anti-progress irrationalism. Neither exists here. The irrational is faced, unmasked, and we discover that for Julien there is no limitation.

With <u>Hérodias</u> we are back in the more familiar realm of limitation. Religion is the consuming courtesan in this story when Hérodias has John the Baptist killed. The story is frankly irrational but it cannot be dismissed as merely that. It deals with the depths of human evil where neither striving nor rationality prevails.

Flaubert gives us another view of striving and rationality in <u>Bouvard et Pécuchet</u>--this time of their ineffectuality. Although the characters are set in a historical context, they are less thoroughly drawn than any of Flaubert's others. They are reminiscent of the half-real, half-mythological figures in <u>Salammbô</u>, though not without sympathy. In <u>Bouvard et Pécuchet</u>, Flaubert explicitly intends and accomplishes the artistic diatribe against the century's follies which fills his letters. His funny-sad protagonists (perhaps he understood them as types) aspire successively to all realms of human knowledge. The results are failure, disillusion, boredom. In imagining that they can master all knowledge and their subsequent disillusion, Bouvard and Pécuchet are not even as self-conscious as Frédéric or Emma. Lack of this self-conscious quality is a central limitation in all Flaubert's characters except Julien, but nowhere else do we have a pair of unconscious pawns for characters. In making Bouvard and Pécuchet thus, Flaubert is commenting on his century's follies and perhaps humanity's as well.[50] His intent is less to create believable people than to dramatize the foibles and weaknesses of all people.

Taken with his <u>Dictionnaire des idées reçues</u> (like <u>Saint Antoine</u> a lifelong project), Flaubert's last and unfinished novel, on one level, adds up to a catalog of ideas, specifically nineteenth-century ideas. The <u>Dictionnaire</u> is especially biting toward progress and materialistic preoccupations. Flaubert defines materialism in these terms: "Prononcer ce mot avec horreur en appuyant sur chaque syllabe."[51] An optimist is equivalent to an imbecile; poetry is useless, poets dreamers; and progress always badly understood and too hasty.[52] Publicity is the source of fortune and rime never accords with reason.[53] The brief work is a priceless insight into Flaubert's attitudes toward his century. On another level, we have Bouvard and Pécuchet returning finally to their copy work, perhaps more self-conscious at last. Knowledge has been illusory, beyond their grasp. They are as limited as Emma, Frédéric, Félicité, but there is a note of sadness (or perhaps merely resignation) which no other work of Flaubert carries. Through Bouvard and Pécuchet, Flaubert says more obviously than through any other characters that limitless human aspirations collide constantly with limited human nature. Man is not Faust.

In all these novels, evil and limitation are not eliminated by striving--the anti-Romantic side of Flaubert's anti-Faust. On the other hand, the novel deals explicitly with irrationality, undermining the very possibility of progress. In Flaubert's perceptions of people and his century recorded in his novelistic worlds, art is more than simply a refuge from savagery and foolishness. His characters live by their illusions, pointing up for us human limitation, irrationality, imperfectibility; they show us finally how Flaubert's art is also the realm of the anti-Faust. For Flaubert art is a theodicy in an entirely different way than for Baudelaire. The poet's concern is with the conjuncture of good and evil, their interlacing in any human situation; the novelist's is with illusion and imperfectibility which cannot be removed from human experience. These are not moral evils, but they bring us close to Baudelaire's views on original sin. Because illusion and imperfectibility exist, utopia is impossible. Flaubert's theodicy justifies evil as a fundamental lack in the human person. None of his characters are monsters of depravity (perhaps Hannon in Salammbô comes closest). They are the funny/sad/limited protagonists we all know and are. They live by their illusions and this in itself explains why there cannot be progress for any of them, Julien alone excepted. For all Flaubert's other characters, illusion and limitation are the indispensable parts of their lives, explaining why their existences remain unassimilated, a series of discrete moments. Julien alone becomes part of a larger belief system, perhaps indicating that Flaubert continued to reserve a tiny corner for the persistence of religious ideals. When the prevailing ethos was Christian (or at least religious in some extended sense), limitation was explained by human distance from God and justified by man's lack of knowledge of God's wisdom or of ultimate redemption of the world. In the desacralized nineteenth century, Baudelaire considers limitation in the conjuncture of good and evil. As quasi-evils, the limitations of sadness and memory, among others, create the evil, mysterious face of life which makes art. For Flaubert, limitation is an aspect of illusion, the part of human existence most necessary to his characters. When their illusions die, they too must die.

Both writers offer an antidote to desacralization and to theories of progress, though Flaubert specifically opposes the socialists of his day more vehemently than Baudelaire did. Because he does not believe that limitation is removed by striving, Flaubert is an anti-Romantic figure. Except for Julien, his characters do not grow. He carries anti-Romanticism even further in denying the very possibility of human development. In all his letters, there is only one curious passage referring to evolutionary possibilities for humanity, and this merely in a context of noting that democracy is not the final political stage.[54] Flaubert is an anti-Enlightenment figure because he allows little psychic space for rationality. He reorders the desacralized reality by restoring (and focusing almost exclusively on) its limited, irrational side. His characters operate through a variety of motives, mostly unconscious, but they are models of irrationality, rather than its opposite.

Flaubert's people need innocence, too, but unlike Baudelaire's or Gautier's creation of the dream world of restored innocence, Flaubert seems to deny its possibility. Except for Julien, his protagonists never recapture innocence, and however kindly Flaubert may have drawn Félicité, Un coeur simple also comments on what Flaubert thought of her type of innocence. The bird/Spirit confusion is not unkindly delineated. It does not need to be. To his century Flaubert implies that Fourier's phalansteries and the St.-Simonian ideal will never restore innocence. The limited, foolish human heart is the fundamental starting point and problem. Utopia can offer no new religion.

Nor are limitation and folly susceptible to assimilation. Brombert argues that Flaubert's characters all live in an atmosphere of nonassimilated reality, that the novelist's pessimism is "an indignation in the face of reality so cluttered it leaves no room for meaning."[55] In addition to renewing innocence, religion had previously served this integrating function. Only the alternative world of art can now offer not a religion but a theodicy for these things. In an unintelligible, fragmented world, only the limited and illusory moments themselves can impart a kind of intelligibility. They create art and, in turn, are preserved in art. Whereas Baudelaire's world is an integrated one by restoration of its evil half, Flaubert's is not--however reordered it may be. This is a fundamental divergence between them as types of the anti-Faust. Baudelaire justifies ineradicable evil, even the undesirability of eliminating it; Flaubert places evil and limitation within a discontinuous reality in which their justification arises from the degree of intelligibility they are able to give separateness itself. Both writers create an allegory for what the societal demise of religion had done to European culture.

The anti-Faust restores evil, limitation, foolishness, justifying their place in human life and, at the same time, offering an artistic antidote to all notions of perfectibility. He performs a quasi-religious function--one leading not to secular redemption (implying transcendence of limitation), but to further immersion in the intractable human condition. Perhaps Goethe's Faust could live only in a post-Renaissance period infatuated with human possibility. The anti-Faust found a true spiritual home in the nineteenth century.

Notes to Chapter IV

[1]All references to Flaubert's correspondence are taken from Oeuvres complètes, 16 vols. (Paris: Club de l'Honnête Homme, 1971-75). Correspondence comprises vols. 12 through 16. Hereafter, only the volume, page, and recipient will be cited. Dates, or partial dates, given in brackets are those of the editor.

Examples of diatribes toward the bourgeoisie abound in Flaubert's letters. Among the more striking are those to George Sand, [10 mai 1867], XIV, 351; to Louis Bouilhet, 4 septembre 1850, XIII, 76; and to Ernest Chevalier [2 septembre 1843], XII, 429.

[2]To Louis Bouilhet, 4 septembre 1850, XIII, 76.

[3]To Louis Bouilhet, 19 décembre 1850, XIII, 109; to Louise Colet, [19 mars 1854], XIII, 476; to Louise Colet [29 janvier 1854], XIII,463; to Louis Bouilhet, 14 novembre 1850, XIII, 94. On action's distastefulness to Flaubert, see the letter to Louise Colet, [5-6 mars 1853], XIII, 297 f.

[4]To Louise Colet, [26-27 mai 1853], XIII, 346 f.

[5]To Louise Colet, [15-16 mai 1852], XIII, 193.

[6]Ibid. See also the letter to Louise Colet, [septembre 1853], XIII, 412, re socialism. These theories are elaborated in many other letters. See those to Mlle Leroyer de Chantepie, [30 mars 1859], XIII, 570; to Amélie Bosquet, [juillet 1864], XIV, 209; to George Sand,[12 juin 1867], XIV, 358; to Louise Colet, [2 juillet 1853], XIII, 370; and to Mme Roger de Genettes [été 1864], XIV, 211. For Flaubert's views on universal suffrage specifically, see the letters to George Sand, 4 ou 5 octobre [1871; dated by René Descharmes], XV, 44; and to George Sand, [30 décembre 1873], XV, 278.

[7]To Tourgueneff, 13 [novembre 1872], XV, 181.

[8]To Louise Colet, [4 septembre 1852], XIII, 233.

[9]To Louise Colet, [19 juin 1852], XIII, 205.

[10]To Louise Colet, [26-27 mai 1853], XIII, 347 f.

[11]To Mlle Leroyer de Chantepie, 18 février 1859, XIII, 661.

[12]The cartoon may have referred also to Saint-Beuve's comment that Flaubert wielded the pen as if it were a scalpel.

[13]<u>Re</u> enlarging the spirit and heart, see the letter to Mlle Leroyer de Chantepie, 23 octobre 1863, XIV, 179. Also see the letter to Mme Roger de Genettes [été 1864], XIV, 210 f.

[14]To his niece Caroline [12 septembre 1866], XIV, 292. <u>Re</u> the conscience of the age and a sampling of his many references to the ivory tower, see the letters to Mlle Leroyer de Chantepie, 23 janvier 1866, XIV, 264; and to George Sand, 8 septembre [1871], XV, 40.

[15]To Mme Roger des Genettes, [12 ou 19 janvier 1878], XVI, 31 f.

[16]To Louise Colet [4 septembre 1852], XIII, 232 f., and to Louise Colet, [5-6 mars 1853], XIII, 298.

[17]To Amélie Bosquet [juillet 1864], XIV, 209.

[18]To Mme Roger des Genettes [décembre 1864], XIV, 223.

[19]On the world as materialistic and hideous, see the letters to Claudius Popelin, [28 octobre 1870], XIV, 604; and to his niece Caroline [28 octobre 1870], XIV, 603. The latter also contains the reference to himself as the mandarin. Discussions of the world as simply ugly are too frequent to cite.

[20]To the Princess Mathilde, 4 mars [1871], XIV, 624.

[21]For the quote, see the letter to George Sand, [début de mars 1872], XV, 110; on human sympathy, the letter to George Sand, [10 août 1868], XIV, 434; and

re government vs. the writer, to Guy de Maupassant, 19 [16] février, 1880, XVI, 327.

[22]To Louise Colet [juin 1852], XIII, 207; to Louise Colet, [31 mars 1853], XIII, 319; to Mlle Leroyer de Chantepie [30 mars 1857], XIII, 570.

[23]Gustave Flaubert, "Les arts et le commerce," Oeuvres complètes, XII, 20, 23. Re "making us dream," see the letter to Louise Colet [26 août 1853], XIII, 399.

[24]To the Princess Mathilde, [2 décembre 1868], XIV, 457.

[25]On the necessity of making art for itself alone, among many such statements in Flaubert's letters, see the following: to his niece Caroline, [18 décembre 1877], XVI, 28; to Louise Colet [début novembre 1851], XIII, 150; and to Louise Colet [30 mai 1852], XIII, 198. Re the necessity of "absorbing the object," see the letter to Louise Colet, [7-8 juillet 1853], XIII, 374. On impersonality in art generally, see the following: to Louise Colet [6 juillet 1852], XIII, 217; to Louise Colet, [24 avril 1852], XIII, 185 f.; and to Louise Colet, [6 novembre 1853], XIII, 428 f. Re schools of art, again examples abound. See the following: to Guy de Maupassant, [25 décembre 1876], XV, 516; to Tourgueneff, 8 [décembre 1877], XVI, 24; to Léon Hennique, 3 [février 1880], XVI, 308; and to Louise Colet [25-26 juin 1853], XIII, 365.

[26]To Louise Colet [27 mars 1852], XIII, 174; to Louise Colet [23 octobre 1853], XIII, 423; to Louise Colet [22 avril 1854], XIII, 487.

[27]To Léon Hennique, 3 [février 1880], XVI, 310.

[28]To Ernest Chevalier, 26 décembre 1838, XII, 351.

[29]To Louise Colet [16 septembre 1853], XIII, 409.

[30]To Louise Colet [16 janvier 1852], XIII, 158.

[31]To Mlle Leroyer de Chantepie, 18 mars [1857], XIII, 567; to Amélie Bosquet [20 août 1866], XIV, 287.

[32]To George Sand [décembre 1875, après le 20], XV, 430 f.

[33]To Edouard Gachot, 23 septembre 1879, XVI, 252 f.

[34]To Louise Colet, [30 septembre 1853], XIII, 417.

[35]To Louise Colet, [7 avril 1854], XIII, 480.

[36]To Louise Colet, [18 septembre 1846], XII, 527; see also the letters to Mlle Leroyer de Chantepie, [12 décembre 1857], XIII, 617, and to Louise Colet [7 septembre 1853], XIII, 406.

[37]To Hippolyte Taine, [fin novembre 1866], XIV, 312; to Hippolyte Taine, 1er décembre [1866], XIV, 313 f.

[38]To Louise Colet, [6 août 1846], XII, 478; to Louise Colet, [5 septembre 1846], XII, 514.

[39]To Louise Colet, [14 août 1853], XIII, 384.

[40]To Louis Bouilhet, 27 juin [1859], XIII, 53; to Louise Colet, [16 août 1853], XIII, 387; to Louis Bouilhet, [20 septembre 1855], XIII, 515.

[41]To Louise Colet, [17 mai 1853], XIII, 342.

[42]To Guy de Maupassant, 19 [16] février 1880, XVI, 327.

[43]To Mme *** [février 1867], XIV, 329; to George Sand, [décembre 1866?]. XIV, 317, and especially the letter to Louise Colet, [24 avril 1852], XIII, 184.

[44]Flaubert, "Les arts et le commerce," p. 20.

[45]To Mlle Leroyer de Chantepie, 18 mai [1857], XIII, 581; to Alfred de Poittevin, 13 mai [1845], XII, 449; to Louise Colet, [24 avril 1852], XIII, 185, among numerous other examples.

[46]Gustave Flaubert, La Première éducation sentimentale, in Oeuvres complètes VIII, 199 ff.

[47]Rudolf Otto, The Idea of the Holy, trans. John W. Harvey (New York, 1970), pp. 12 ff., 31 ff.

[48]Brombert, Flaubert, (Paris, 1971), "Écrivains de toujours" series. pp. 73, 177.

[49]Gustave Flaubert, La tentation de Saint Antoine, (Paris, 1971), p. 219.

[50]There is no question that this was Flaubert's intent. He refers to Bouvard et Pécuchet as "une espèce d'encyclopédie de la Bêtise modern" in a letter to the Vicomtesse Lepic [octobre 1872], XV, 174, and in a similar vein to Mme Brainne, 5 octobre [1872], XV, 170. To Turgenev, he writes of "mes deux idiots. J'ai peur d'en être un moi-même. Quel bouquin!" [27 juillet 1877], XV, 582.

[51]Gustave Flaubert, "Dictionnaire des idées reçues," Bouvard et Pécuchet (Paris, 1966), p. 367.

[52]Ibid., p. 373.

[53]Ibid., p. 374.

[54]To Mlle Leroyer de Chantepie, 18 mai [1857], XIII, 582.

[55]Victor Brombert, The Novels of Flaubert: A Study of Themes and Techniques (Princeton, 1966), pp. 285 f.

CHAPTER V

THÉOPHILE GAUTIER: ART AS ENCHANTMENT

At first meeting, Théophile Gautier is the Faustian re-enchanter. Gautier spans a large portion of nineteenth-century French literary history, incorporating in his work tenets of both Romanticism and "l'art pour l'art," a term he first popularized with his 1834 preface to Mademoiselle de Maupin. In his youth, Gautier was the proverbial "bad boy' of French letters, hurling invectives against the bourgeoisie and acting out his defiance. Later in life, mellowed by the necessities of almost thirty years of journalistic production to support himself and his family, and by his own ambivalence toward industrial progress, Gautier became a softer figure. If there is one consistent strand in his character, it is that he never forsook his dream world. Though Gautier wrote in many genres, he always seemed most at home with various manifestations of the dream world he himself created. For Gautier, reality was not desacralized in some profound, barely understandable sense, but merely disenchanted. The distinction is fundamental.

In the desacralized world of Baudelaire and Flaubert, art offers an areligious explanation for evil, limitation, and folly, opposing both Romantic and Enlightenment solutions to the flight of God/gods from the world. Baudelaire and Flaubert are the anti-Fausts who recognize implicitly that the world had once been sacred. For Gautier, it had merely housed a variety of spirits whose presence ought to be reconjured but whose departure need not be explained. For this reason, Gautier misses the cultural crisis of desacralization, however much he reorders reality. In Gautier's dream world, evil and limitation exist, but on their own, very different terms, transformed into the strangely manageable world of the dream. Substitution is made for the dark face of life in a dreamed darkness. Sadness lies more in the missed dream than in any real condition. But Gautier cannot be easily dismissed.

Although he is the Faustian re-enchanter singing of other realities, he is also, with Baudelaire and Flaubert, an anti-Romantic and anti-Enlightenment figure. Romantic striving leads to the dream world, close to and inseparable from the real world, but fulfillment exists in neither. Furthermore, in spite of Gautier's interest in the future, his intellectual position is basically in opposition to Enlightenment rationalism. The dream world of art is a necessary antidote to reality itself, creating a more inclusive illusion than for Baudelaire or Flaubert, and perhaps for this reason less cogent.

Gautier's world of illusion is built upon well-delineated theories of art. Central to these is the dichotomy between the real and the ideal which is blurred in art. In his major short stories, much of his poetry and travel literature, even in his journalism, Gautier creates ideal figures who transcend human contingencies. In his short stories and novels, these are almost always women; in his poetry, the ideal is the world of art; in his travel literature and journalism, the artistic dream.

"Spirite" is perhaps the most famous of Gautier's short stories, and especially significant for his theories of art because it was published in 1865 toward the end of his life. From the initial warning of a friend that "the spirits have an eye on you,"[1] Gautier's protagonist is swept into an ideal/real dichotomy which is progressively blurred. When the lovely Spirite who inhabits the earth but is neither demon nor angel avows her love for Guy, their union seems initially impossible. Disappointed, she enters a convent and "dies" there, then returns to earth as the invisible witness to Guy's life. When he discovers her grave and name, the rest of his life is lived in two existences, the real and the fantastic, until Spirite contrives his death so that his wish to join her can be fulfilled. Beneath the gothic trappings and contrivances, the story says much about Gautier's views of art. His character returns at one point to a Paris peopled with the living dead because they lack an interior life.[2] Beneath the usual macabre Gautier fixtures, the ideal and real worlds are indistinguishable. Access to the ideal is gained through art and death. The theme of innocence is likewise strong, provided by contact with the dream world and ultimately by death when Guy can no longer live in an even slightly dichotomized world.

An equally strong case for the function of art as blurring the distinction between the real and the ideal can be made from other stories in the same collection, Contes fantastiques. In "Arria Marcella," Octavian's desire for the beautiful Pompeiian gives her life again. Apparently Gautier toyed with a similar idea for a ballet even at the very end of his life. The plot for this was to revolve around a young artist's love for a statue of Venus which would breathe life into the marble.[3] In "Giselle" the opposite occurs when the ideal figure saves the real.[4] The spiritualized Giselle rescues Albert from the Wilis so that he has both life and the remembrance of an idealized love. The point is not to view Gautier as the perpetual adolescent in these evocations, but for the moment merely to establish the blur his art creates of reality and illusion. The dream world becomes even more literal for Gautier in "Le pied de momie."[5] His protagonist buys the foot of a mummified princess, then journeys with her to Egypt to find another gift in return for the foot, and ends with a small figurine really standing on his dresser. "La morte amoureuse"[6] leads the reader to wonder whether the story involves a priest who dreams he is a seigneur or vice versa. We need not go to Contes fantastiques alone in search of such deliberate confusion. In the Jeunes france collection, Gautier creates Elias Wildmanstadius, a man of the Middle Ages trapped in the nineteenth century who takes a cathedral for his mistress and dies when she is struck by thunder.[7] And there is one of the most famous novels of the nineteenth century, Mademoiselle de Maupin,[8] famous for its antibourgeois preface and its catalogue of degeneracy designed to shock the bourgeoisie. Whatever else it may be, the novel itself, not merely the preface, says a great deal about Gautier's theories of art. Maupin is Gautier's solution to the problem of the ideal lover, an androgynous figure skillfully playing between reality and illusion. When the ideal has been realized, Maupin leaves.

All this could be viewed as silly, and it is deceptively easy to dismiss Gautier for this, among many other reasons. But when we prescind from the gothic formula and elements which can only be kindly described as juvenile, Gautier's central theory of art emerges. Art's purpose is to create an ideal world; the blurring of reality is essential to this purpose. In the ideal world, beauty alone is worshipped. Beauty alone transcends all human contingencies,[9] and transforms the ordinary in a way we might not choose but find difficult to ignore in Gautier's theories of art. Beauty is almost as central to these theories as the creation of illusion.

Gautier often described art as beauty itself,[10] and Baudelaire described Gautier as the "perfect man of letters" for his exclusive love of beauty, in Maupin, for instance, creating a style appropriate for the enthusiasm (as distinguished from the passion) created by beauty.[11] Gautier wrote frequently of how he had searched for beauty under all its Protean forms in nature and the arts, finding man alone ugly.[12] His ideal love figures are also ideal beauty figures, and we need not go far to hear Gautier's denunciations of bourgeois usefulness, even to the extent that when a thing becomes useful it ceases to be beautiful.[13] Beauty's fecundity is celebrated in many of Gautier's poems; for example, in "Le poète et la foule," and in "La source" as explicitly as anywhere in his poetry.

> Tout près du lac filtre une source,
> Entre deux pierres, dans un coin;
> Allégrement l'eau prend sa course
> Comme pour s'en aller bien loin.
>
> Elle murmure: 'Oh! quelle joie
> Sous la terre il faisait si noir!
> Maintenant ma rive verdoie,
> Le ciel se mire à mon miroir.'[14]

In "Premier sourire du printemps," the month of March secretly prepares for spring, perhaps as the poet secretly conjures beauty.

> Puis lorsque sa besogne est faite,
> Et que son règne va finir,
> Au seuil d'avril tournant la tête,
> Il dit: 'Printemps, tu peux venir!'[15]

If these themes sound Romantic, there are many such overtones in Gautier's poetry. The soul is described in a mortal cage and entombed in winter's death.[16] The poet is a captive bird in "Ce que disent les hirondelles," but without the evocative power of Baudelaire's albatross. The most famous of Gautier's poems in Emaux et camées explores the theme that art alone is eternal.

> Tout passe. --L'art robuste
> Seul a l'éternité.
> Le buste
> Survit à la cité.
>
> Et la médaille austère
> Que trouve un laboureur
> Sous terre
> Révèle un empereur.
>
> Les dieux eux-mêmes meurent.
> Mais les vers souverains
> Demeurent
> Plus forts que les airains.
>
> Sculpte, lime cisèle;
> Que ton rêve flottant
> Se scelle
> Dans le bloc résistant![17]

Perhaps no more explicit statement of art's eternity could be found, nor of the artistic dream "sealed" into its medium. Romantic themes in Gautier's poetry also include his celebration of both the grotesque and the ordinary. Emaux et camées contains poems praising the human hand, a red dress, the contralto voice ("bizarre mélange, Hermaphrodite de la voix")[18] and blackbirds. But "Symphonie en blanc majeur" exhibits an interest like Baudelaire's in synesthesia, finally concluding in a similar artistic manner to Whistler's experiments with white and color:

> Oh! qui pourra mettre un ton rose
> Dans cette implacable blancheur![19]

The beauty of art is not unalloyed for Gautier. True art should admit both the tragic and the comic faces of life. The fantastic, the trivial, the ignoble--all have their place in art, because life itself is multiple (and, as we will see, Gautier's art is often profoundly connected with life in spite of his protestations to the contrary), and because as

Gautier says, without the demon the angel would have no value either.[20] Gautier's _Les grotesques_ concretizes this concern for the fantastic and trivial in his reexamination of poets who had been considered second-rate in previous centuries. If tragedy and comedy seem too absolute in their exclusiveness for Gautier, perhaps the same point might be made for his perceptions of reality and illusion. And, though art elevates the ordinary, he thinks it should exist by itself, outside philosophy or history.[21]

Gautier's article "Du beau dans l'art" explores his theories of beauty as fully as any of his writings. Each poet or artist carries his secret with him, an ideal type of beauty existing in his spirit. The artist takes from nature what he needs to express this, making of the canvas an intermediary between himself and nature. For this reason there can be no "progress" in art because each poet is an original.[22] These statements come close to expressing the poetic unity of the thing seen and the seer, much as Baudelaire's _flâneur_ pose united the world outside with the observer who was ultimately indistinguishable from that world. Yet Gautier also urges in the 1832 preface to his poetry that the artist should have no political color and apparently scant connectedness with life.[23]

These ideas lead us directly to a problem focal to any adequate understanding of Gautier; namely, the contradictions in his theories of beauty. He can sound at times like Flaubert searching for ideal beauty, or, alternately, like Baudelaire admiring the dress and smile of his own century. The question of art's relation to life is especially significant in Gautier's case because it bears directly on the more central issue of reality and illusion, of which these theories of beauty form only a part. Gautier's urgings that art must be practiced for its own sake are carried furthest in the prefaces to _Maupin_ and the 1832 edition of his poetry. In the former, Gautier claims that the truly beautiful serves no purpose whatever. The useful is ugly because it is the expression of some need, usually a need as ignoble and distasteful as man's poor and infirm nature. Joy is life's purpose and the only useful thing in the world.[24] In the preface to his poetry, Gautier asserts that in general when a thing becomes useful, it ceases to be beautiful.

These posturings are typical, though somewhat extreme, in the "l'art pour l'art" tradition. There is a superior world of art which need serve no purpose other than its own existence; art alone is eternal; the bourgeoisie (of whom Gautier speaks at length in the Maupin preface) is inherently incapable of appreciating true beauty. Because Gautier was so violently antibourgeois in his early years and came to epitomize for the generation of 1830 the artist in revolt against society, these antibourgeois views are worth documenting further. In "Sous la table" from Les jeunes france, Gautier's character Roderic claims that "la vertu n'est pas un nom, mais un non," and that virtue is saying "no" to all that is agreeable in life, ending only in hypocrisy and falsehood.[25] In "Daniel Jovard" from the same collection, Daniel is a representative of the crowd, "a type of the non-type," fossilized and antediluvian, who "acquited himself classically of all the functions of life".[26] Another of Gautier's characters falls in love with a woman who turns out to be as bourgeois as Gautier can imagine: she worries over a broken comb in a moment of passion, and her husband allows the story's protagonist to trifle with his wife in an extraordinary display of bourgeois obtuseness. Then in the typically impertinent fashion of his early days Gautier explains the story as an allegory of Romantic vs. Classical poetry, in case the bourgeois reader has missed the point.[27] Years later Gautier referred to his youthful scorn for the bourgeoisie, which was almost everyone. Drunk with art, passion, and poetry, the young managed to survive their world: "The destiny of Icarus frightened no one. . . ."[28]

Gautier felt all his life that poets were among the least encouraged members of society. A father's first prayer was that his child not be a poet.[29] And as for the difference between poetry and prose, Gautier viewed the former as a "disdainful mistress for whom one ruins oneself"; and the latter as "an honest woman who nourishes."[30] Apparently he felt the pull between the two most keenly when he returned from his travels in Spain in 1840 to settle into what became thirty years of almost weekly journalistic production which Gautier never found artistically fulfilling. "Adieux à la poésie" speaks of the necessities of falling into prose and concludes:

> O pauvre enfant du ciel, tu chanterais en vain:
> Ils ne comprendraient pas ton langage divin;
> A tes plus doux accords leur oreille est fermée!
>
> Mais, avant de partir, mon bel ange à L'oeil bleu,
> Va trouver de ma part ma pâle bien-aimée,
> Et pose sur son front un long baiser d'adieu![31]

We have met similar, though less violently expressed, ideas in Baudelaire and Flaubert. How seriously or consistently these ideas were practiced is an entirely different question. They become puzzling in Gautier when juxtaposed with some of his other writings on art. When Gautier became editor-in-chief of <u>L'Artiste</u> in 1856, he acquired the ideal forum for expressing the other side of his artistic views which he developed during the last two decades of his life. According to this side, the artist is above all a man who should reflect in his work the passions, beliefs, and prejudices of his time. Art is play, fancy, compensation for life, a vital component of everyday living. In the prospectus for <u>L'Artiste</u>, Gautier explains his hopes that the magazine will examine, among other things, the facade of a house, a clock, a lamp, feminine style, transportation vehicles, and elegant home interiors: "Everything that form touches is our province."[32] Gautier thinks Paris can become the new Rome, and in other articles he discusses modern streets, railroads, and art for the masses. Talent can make a new thing of a banal subject.[33] Perhaps Gautier had something like this in mind when he wrote of railroad stations as the "cathedrals of the future" and the possibility of art for the masses which would inculcate the "moral power of beauty."[34] If we can believe Gautier's statements that the poet's function is to give body to an idea, that the poet like Antaeus should touch the earth from time to time,[35] Gautier is preeminently opposed to abstractions. We have seen much of this in <u>Emaux et camées</u>. Then the question of morality in art becomes for Gautier a question of elevating people through the admiration of beauty (as in his assertions that the public be exposed to opera),[36] rather than a religious or social question. The reverse side of elevating the public is stopping the "mounting sea of modern barbarism." Poetry is thus more useful than religion, law, or industry. On the question of poetry for the working class, Gautier has much to say in his later life. Manual and intellectual labor are not incompatible, he thinks, and in fact manual labor can be more favorable to poetry than journalism. Gautier views social inequality as a fatal law, but poetry for the workers should be simply poetry, without social trappings, not a consolation nor mere amusement, but a true elevation of the human spirit.[37]

All this hardly sounds like the rabid Gautier of younger days eager to excoriate the bourgeoisie. Judged from the perspective of his life work, it is impossible to avoid the conclusion that after his youthful rebellion, Gautier came to terms with his century's industrial and increasingly bourgeois character. By the 1850's perhaps from a combination of economic necessity and genuine intellectual conviction, Gautier was more interested in educating the bourgeois than in denouncing him. He is, of course, still capable of the latter, as an 1856 letter to Flaubert attests in which he speaks of bourgeois stupidity.[38] But Gautier's idea of the artist became basically a notion of his civilizing mission, fused with the tenets of "l'art pour l'art" to which he himself had made a considerable contribution. By the end of Gautier's life it was possible for him to speak both of the obtuseness of bourgeois life and the necessity of educating the public in art. In spite of Baudelaire's avowal that Gautier keeps his true thoughts to himself and does not really praise "Msgr. Progrès et . . . très-puissante dame Industrie,"[39] whatever his initial motivation, Gautier was a man profoundly interested in his century. He speaks of the speed of modern life and the evocative power of poetry, often in the same article.[40] In his preface to the 1869 edition of <u>Les fleurs du mal</u>, he highlights Baudelaire's horror of progress, utilitarianism, utopian thought, but also Baudelaire's power to evoke an unknown world, a chorus of mysterious ideas. In this power of evocation, the object is transformed, both in itself and for the public. The purpose of a painting is not merely to mirror objects like a photograph, but like the statues of Praxiteles and Phidias, to be both "admirable" and "false,"[41] a statement as clear as anything even Baudelaire wrote on the artificiality of art. For Gautier, too, in spite of his concern for public appreciation of art, the artist always remained an artistocrat in an increasingly unaristocratic age. And, though he never adopted a Baudelairean pose, there is something of the _flâneur_ as well in Gautier.

Alongside elitist views of the artist in society, Gautier's work also speaks to the peculiar dilemmas of modern life. However much he eschewed utilitarianism and St.-Simonian perfectibility,[42] Gautier believed in the possibility of progress. He parted company with Flaubert and Baudelaire, on the one hand, when he admitted this possibility, and with the utopians on the other, because he did not believe in a static state of perfection. In spite of his interest in and support for the decorative and practical arts, Gautier feared materialistic encroachments, arguing with Baudelaire that the effect of all extreme civilization is to substitute the material for the spiritual, the thing for the idea. Once in viewing the decline of a civilization, he refused to believe in any progress at all.[43] Even apparent progress could be deceptive. Among the greatest unhappinesses of modern life, for example, Gautier included lack of adventure because chance was no longer possible. In his view, everything was too well-ruled to the detriment of human will. Gloomily, he foresaw a day of numerous suicides when curiosity, the principal moving power of life, would be extinguished.[44] Obviously, his own taste for adventure dictated these views. For Gautier, the greatest pleasure in travel was the process of getting there, not the arrival.[45]

Set alongside Baudelaire and Flaubert, Théophile Gautier is indeed a contradictory figure. Although he was the first to use the term "l'art pour l'art' in any general sense (unlike Keats, who spoke of poetry as an end in itself as early as 1818 in England), it cannot be maintained that this was either his consistent view or practice. In fact, Gautier's interest for the student of "l'art pour l'art" solely from the aspect of literary theory is that he found art both related and nonrelated to life. He thundered against the bourgeoisie, then proceeded to argue for their education in the arts and to focus the editorial policy of a major artistic journal in this direction. Gautier was neither the purist of his early years nor of Baudelaire's description of him as the "perfect man of letters." He was neither a poet comparable to Baudelaire nor a novelist the equal of Flaubert. He did write some highly original poetic pieces, mostly in their choice of subjects; some immensely entertaining stories; and a huge body of easily forgettable and difficult to trace journalistic production. It has been estimated that if all Gautier's diverse works in numerous genres were collected, they would fill over three hundred volumes.

Within the context of "l'art pour l'art," whereas Flaubert and Baudelaire restore limitation and darkness, Gautier creates an entirely new world. He is a Faustian re-enchanter, an all-powerful Earth Spirit who conjures up other realities. Everything becomes for him a species of dream. In Contes fantastiques this is most obvious. The real/ideal worlds of his characters are virtually indistinguishable, and, as we have seen, this seems to be Gautier's intent. Life itself becomes dream. Emaux et camées conjures up entire worlds from subjects like hands and a red dress. All Gautier's art criticism can be read as an attempt to explain how the poet or painter creates dream. Even his travel literature, his Spanish poems, and the journal of his travels express regret for the lost dream. This is stated explicitly at the end of Tra los montes when the poet's tears upon reaching his own country are not those of the joyful pilgrim returned, but of regret because the dream has ended.[46] Reality has an imperious quality for Gautier and perhaps for this reason he prefers to fill it with spirits answerable to himself rather than to explain its harshness. Even questions of evil are integrated into the dream world in a manageable way. The bohemian poet Onuphrius from the Jeunes france collection is driven mad, but from watching a young dandy eat poetic verses which are suspended in a kind of gelatin.[47] The effect of this strange death is to blur the fact of death itself. The evil done to the young man becomes manageable when nothing else in the story makes sense either. The same comment can be made of all Gautier's creatures who make excursions into the spirit world. If we suspend disbelief completely, Spirite is able to communicate with Guy through writing, Giselle can save her beloved from the Wilis, and a statue can become alive. In only one of Gautier's stories does evil become what it is--an irrational incursion into life inseparable from good. In "Deux acteurs pour un rôle" the young actor realizes that the devil has played the role of Mephistopheles.[48] For Gautier, the spirits (God himself) were harmful, man's enemies. According to an early biographer, Gautier "was not superstitious; he was superstition itself."[49] Apparently, the spirits could be controlled only when the dream world was made manageable through art. In the dream world of art, evil and limitation exist, but on their own, very different terms. They are not, as for Baudelaire and Flaubert basically unintelligible because the world has been permanently and totally desacralized. The absence of God/gods does not need as much to be explained as does the world filled with new presences.

Viewed as the Faustian re-enchanter who had power to conjure up an alternative world, Gautier is as utopian as anyone he denounced. Filling the world with new gods does not explain the departure of the old ones. Sadness for the lost dream, as in "Giselle" or "La morte amoureuse," does not compare with Baudelaire's expressions of the sad and sinful human condition, or Flaubert's of its inherent limitation. Gautier remains locked in himself, a fact Flaubert criticizes in his characters by implication. Perhaps Gautier always remained, too, the ecstatic "twenty-year-old poet," as one detractor asserted.[50] For Flaubert's characters, no ecstasy lasts, even for Félicité, though Julien is perhaps an exception. Gautier's characters enter an ecstatic world and live there in a substitute life. His poetic themes, too, create an alternative world. In his journalism alone Gautier is forced to deal with the present reality, and we can only imagine how difficult constant journalistic necessities must have been for this man who so ardently desired to create dream. His theoretical interest in the artistic dream suffuses even his journalism, though, and these writings contain the bulk of his literary theories. Practice took entirely different directions, as we have seen.

But Gautier is more than a Faustian re-enchanter. He experiments with a wide range of anti-Romantic themes and new verse forms in L'España and his collected poems. A broader anti-Romantic thrust is in Gautier's idea of striving. Certainly most of his characters could be called Romantic strivers. Even his young bohemians/dandies in Les jeunes france pursue other worlds, and the point is most obvious in Contes fantastiques and Maupin. Yet these are all dream worlds without fulfillment. The ideal/real love is never held, except for a moment in Maupin, and part of that curious novel's message seems to be precisely that the ideal cannot be possessed. If Guy joins Spirite in the end, it is at the sacrifice of his accustomed life for a non-corporeal fulfillment. The priest/seigneur in "La morte amoureuse" finds the love of God an inadequate substitute for the beautiful courtesan Clarimonde. And when the hero of "Arria Marcella" finally marries, his wife knows he loves the Pompeiian, her spirit exorcised in a pile of cinders mixed with a few bones and jewels.[51] There is fulfillment in none of these stories. Instead of a Romantic version of reality in which all is made whole or in which unfulfilled yearning at least makes sense, the dream world becomes a strangely fragmented version of infinite desire doomed to endless and almost absurd repetition. There is an unsettled quality in all Gautier's work. His one-dimensional characters constantly seek the alternative of dream, but on closer examination Romantic striving simply does not exist for them, except in a truncated version having more in common with Flaubert's discontinuous realities than with traditional Romantic notions of unfulfilled yearning.

Paradoxically, because he restores the dream world, Gautier is also an anti-Enlightenment figure. In spite of his ideas about railroad stations as the cathedrals of the future and the ambivalence of his stance toward progress, Gautier's fundamental position is anti-rationalist. For Gautier, art may indeed be connected with life, but dream is his essential world, a necessary substitution for reality itself, hardly a rationalist posture.

As theodicy, dream offers an alternative world in which evil is integral and explained as such, though without the depth of either Baudelaire or Flaubert. The Wilis' threat to sweep Albert into a dance to death is a species of evil. The dandy's treatment of Onuphrius is evil. So is the devil's interpretation of Mephistopheles. Even in Gautier's dream world, evil exists as itself, not merely in interaction with discontent resulting in Faustian striving. Foolishness and limitation exist in the dream world, too. Guy's physical body is a barrier in "Spirite" though eventually overcome, but the point applies to all attempts to reach the dream world. Just as this world itself is doomed to be always desired and never achieved, "Spirite" can be read as a story of limitation. The impossibility of touching creatures from another world unless we ourselves enter that world permeates Gautier's fantastic tales and there are heavy doses of the fantastic in all his stories. Maupin, too, can be seen as a parable of limitation. And all his characters who seek other realities are, almost by definition, a little foolish. Finally, there is restored innocence in the dream world, often as a prerequisite for entry. If death does not reestablish innocence, as in "Spirite", the dream itself does, as in Gautier's poetry or travel literature.

What is missing is connectedness with real life; and this is precisely the distinction between Gautier and his other two greater French contemporaries who face the problem of desacralization. Gautier's world remains basically unattached. Spirite or any other ideal love character does not exist, and we are left with an entire world which has never, and can never, exist. Yet a reordered reality it is, and on a scale of totality which neither Baudelaire nor Flaubert attempted. The totality of the illusion is the unifying principle of Gautier's imaginative work, as well as the underlying reason why he remains merely a re-enchanter, though finally an anti-Faustian one. Taken in their totality, Gautier's worlds of illusion constitute a theodicy, explaining evil and limitation in the dream world and restoring innocence there. But because Gautier's theodicy is unconnected to real life, with the line between reality and dream hopelessly blurred, it finally dissolves into antidote, Gautier's more important anti-Faustian dimension.

"L'art pour l'art" in its most profound meaning for him is "art for enchantment's sake." Like many other "l'art pour l'art" advocates, Gautier sees a rising tide of barbarism and ignorance. Art can educate the bourgeois, create alternative worlds for both artist and people, and (with a heavy interlacing of escapism) provide a kind of secular salvation from barbarism. But at bottom, what Gautier's art cannot do is precisely what Baudelaire's and Flaubert's does: offer a theodicy and an antidote to desacralization, central to the nineteenth-century real world, by restoring the evil and limitation of that world. For Gautier reality remains merely disenchanted. It is the charm and the weakness of his work.

Notes to Chapter V

[1]Théophile Gautier, "Spirite," <u>Contes fantastiques</u> (Paris, 1973), p. 184.

[2]Ibid., p. 277.

[3]Emile Bergerat, <u>Théophile Gautier: entretiens, souvenirs et correspondance</u> (Paris, 1880), pp. 217 ff.

[4]Synopsis for "Giselle" Le ballet du Théâtre National de l'Opéra de Paris, 1978.

[5]"Le Pied de momie," <u>Contes fantastiques.</u>

[6]"La morte amoureuse,"<u>Contes fantastiques</u>.

[7]Théophile Gautier, "Elias Wildmanstadius," <u>Les jeunes france</u> (Paris, 1974), p. 198.

[8]Théophile Gautier, <u>Mademoiselle de Maupin</u> (Paris, 1966).

[9]Théophile Gautier, "Du beau dans l'art," <u>Revue des deux mondes</u> 19 (1847): 904. Reprinted in Théophile Gautier, <u>L'Art Moderne</u> (Paris, 1856).

[10]Théophile Gautier, "La Divine Epopée," <u>Revue des deux mondes</u> 26 (31 mars 1841): 121. Also see "Du beau dans l'art,"<u>Revue des deux mondes</u> 19 (1847): 901; and Bergerat, <u>Théophile Gautier</u>, p. 76.

[11]Charles Baudelaire, "Galerie du XIXe siècle: Théophile Gautier, <u>L'Artiste</u> 6 (13 mars 1859): 164, 170.

[12]Bergerat, <u>Théophile Gautier</u>, p. 128.

[13]<u>Mademoiselle de Maupin</u>, préface, p. 45.

[14]Théophile Gautier, "Le poète et la foule," <u>L'España de Théophile Gautier</u>, édition critique, René Jasinski (Paris, 1929), p. 172. Théophile Gautier, "La source," <u>Emaux et camées</u> (Paris, 1888), p. 121.

[15]"Premier sourire du printemps," <u>Emaux et camées</u>, p. 49.

[16]"Rêve," Poésies 1830-32, in Poésies complètes, I (Paris, 1889), p. 38. "La derniere feuille," Poésies diverses 1833-38, in Poésies complètes, I (Paris, 1889), p. 235.

[17]"L'art," Emaux et camées, pp. 225 f.

[18]"Contralto,"Emaux et camées, p. 53.

[19]"Symphonie en blanc majeur, "Emaux et camées, p. 33.

[20]Théophile Gautier, Les Grotesques, (Paris, 1859), p. 353.

[21]L'Art moderne, p. 237. Also see "École Allemande--Cornelius," L'Artiste 13 (1 décembre 1854): 129.

[22]"Du beau dans l'art,"Revue des deux mondes 19 (1847): 889 f.

[23]Poésies 1830-32, préface, in Poésies complètes, I, 3.

[24]Mademoiselle de Maupin, préface pp. 45 f.

[25]"Sous la table," Les jeunes france, pp. 41 f.

[26]"Daniel Jovard," Les jeunes france, pp. 92, 94.

[27]"Celle-ci et celle-la," Les jeunes france, pp. 149, 164, 192.

[28]Théophile Gautier, Histoire du romantisme (Paris, 1874), pp. 153 f.

[29]Théophile Gautier, "Revue littéraire: poésies nouvelles," Revue des deux mondes 26 (14 juin 1841): 906.

[30]Ibid., p. 906.

[31]"Adieux à la poésie," L'España de Théophile Gautier, p. 269.

[32]"Prospectus" for L'Artiste, 14 décembre 1856, p.3.

[33]Ibid., p. 2. Also see "Théâtres," La Presse 10 janvier 1848 and 20 mars 1848; "Salon de 1848," La Presse, 22 avril 1848, and "Revue des arts," Revue des deux mondes 27 (31 aout 1841).

[34]For "cathedrals of the future" quote, see "Théâtres," La Presse, 10 janvier 1848. Re art for the masses, see "Théâtres," La Presse, 20 mars 1848.

[35]"La Divine Epopée," Revue des deux mondes, 26 (31 mars 1841): 123.

[36]"Théâtres," La Presse, 20 mars 1848.

[37]"Revue littéraire: poésies nouvelles," Revue des deux mondes 26 (14 juin 1841): 912, 914 f. See also "Théâtres," La Presse, 20 mars 1848, and préface, Les fleurs du mal, 2d ed. (Paris,1869), p. 75.

[38]To Gustave Flaubert, 1856, in Les plus belles lettres de Théophile Gautier présentées par Pierre Descaves (Paris, 1962), p. 74.

[39]Charles Baudelaire, "Galerie du XIXe siècle: Théophile Gautier," L'Artiste 6 (13 mars 1859): 170.

[40]"Tableaux de l'école moderne," Le Moniteur universel, 6 février 1860.

[41]"Salon de 1837," La Presse, 11 mars 1837.

[42]Preface to second edition of Les fleurs du mal, p. 19. Also see Gautier's views cited previously in the prefaces to Maupin, and the 1832 edition of his poetry.

[43]Théophile Gautier, Tra los montes: voyage en Espagne (Paris, 1961), p. 326.

[44]Ibid., p. 275.

[45]Ibid., p. 322.

[46] Ibid. p. 395.

[47]"Onuphrius," Les jeunes france, p. 88.

[48]"Deux acteurs pour un rôle," Contes fantastiques.

[49]Bergerat, Théophile Gautier, p. 165.

[50]E. Caro, Etudes morales sur le temps présent (Paris, 1855), p. 213.

[51]"Arria Marcella," Contes fantastiques, p. 163.

CHAPTER VI

THE ENGLISH SCENE

Victorian England in many ways can be seen as a society which accommodated both God and Faust. Far more than in France, elements of Enlightenment rationalism and Romantic striving persisted through an ethos of religion, stability, and progress. That the cultural damages to Christianity could thus be covered by faith in human possibility is a basic distinction between the French and English artistic responses to desacralization. Walter Pater's idea of the peak moments and a return to tradition represent a kind of Faustian striving in their emphasis on possibility, however much his personal stance was that of spectator rather than participant. Pater's world was one of still-realizable possibility. Algernon Charles Swinburne, whose intellectual lineage was in large part French, was not so typical a Victorian as Pater. For Swinburne, experience was discontinuous, bound up with evil and limitation, necessitating the substitute god of art. The social dimension of Swinburne's shrill negativism was based to a great extent on his reactions against progress and rationality in the manner of the French anti-Fausts.

The effect of the Victorian belief in religion, stability, and progress was to mute the cultural crisis of desacralization, ironically enough, chiefly through a multiplication of religious issues. Ultimately, religious losses at the core were masked by an astonishing range of religious concerns at the periphery. Evangelicalism, for example, having early bequeathed to the century a potent mix of social concern and individual importance, imparted along with Methodism a veneer of religiosity to the whole of society. During the 1840's the Oxford Movement centered attention on more specifically ecclesiological concerns when Newman and his followers made the intellectual pilgrimage from High Church observance to Roman Catholicism. In reaction to these issues, the next decades witnessed the prolonged science versus religion conflict after publication of Darwin's Origin of Species in 1859 and Descent of Man in 1871. All these religious interests, as well as great concern in other quarters for a morality separated from religious beliefs, tended to mute desacralization. The veneer of religiosity and morality affected all areas of life. Much more than their French contemporaries, the Victorians analyzed the progress of their age, whose fitting symbol was the Crystal Palace. They found it a transitional period, often failing to meet evangelical standards of morality, often caught up in industrial abuses, but usually enlightened. In art, the religious/moral veneer expressed itself in concern for the moral improvement of society, a viewpoint against which Swinburne reacted most violently, and which is strikingly displayed in Victorian periodical literature, specifically in the innumerable connections made among religion, morality and art. This will be our point of departure for analyzing the English context of "art for art's sake."

Victorian England in general exhibited a concern for connections between literature and life almost like the St.-Simonians in France. The aim of "art for the people," posing an obvious and probably intended foil to the principles of "art for art's sake," was to make people more sensitive to the spiritual world. Through art, contact could be established with the ideal. As one author wrote in an 1886 edition of <u>Macmillan's Magazine</u>:

> Sympathy with our fellow-men, high aspirations, purity, unworldliness, these are the helps to the imagination. Selfishness, unbelief, sensuality, worldliness, these are the hindrances. These are the chains which bind us to the earth, these are the clouds which hide from us the light of heaven.[1]

In another such foil, literature exists for the reader--to please and make him happy, to lighten life's burdens. Therefore, any art which does not express good and noble thought, which "degrades or libels humanity," is "devilish."[2] From Herbert Spencer to the Catholic periodical <u>The Month</u>, the spectrum is complete: literature ought to influence conduct.[3] <u>The Month</u> even maintained the extreme position that for the Christian all art must be characterized by religious feeling. Production of the beautiful is made inseparable from enjoyment and moral rectitude, two themes which recur repeatedly in all this literature.[4] Both are linked specifically to concepts of health, as well as to Ruskin's revival of the Artistotelean idea that art must imitate nature. The novel must purify the mind, improve society, and make the reader happier. As for the artist, Cornhill Magazine, among others, claimed that a "healthy organism," inevitably meaning "moral health," is essential to poetic production.[5]

The opposition to "l'art pour l'art," whose tenets were widely known by the 1870's and 1880's, could hardly be more clearly stated: beauty is not manifold (certainly it could not include Baudelaire's Les fleurs du mal); it provides entree to a rarefied world which then cleanses the real world; it elevates, always in moral and religious terms, both the individual and society. In short, like everything else in the society, it must be useful.

The focus of attack, of course, was France, though Swinburne is often indirectly indicted.[6] As if to prove the poet's point in Notes on Poems and Reviews, one periodical writer actually claims that English novels are specifically written for boys and girls.[7] The startling and the vulgar which many Victorian writers found capsulized in French fiction was considered a danger to "religious belief" and "moral purity."[8] Although these attacks were chiefly against supposedly immoral content in literature, the underlying assumption was that literature should serve moral and instructional purposes, thus involving an attack on the aesthetic principles of "art for art's sake" as well. There were few attempts to cast religious or moral questions within a larger cultural framework. One writer in the Quarterly Review earlier in the century did consider French novels both cause and consequence of a general threat to European society, but then immediately linked lowering of public taste with narrower issues of morality and public safety. The author characterized the fiction of the 1830's (chiefly the novels of Balzac) as extravagant, absurd, and immoral.[9] The prevailing mood had changed little by the 1860's and 1880's when Victorian periodicals consistently viewed French fiction either as morally neutral to its enormous detriment or (more usually) as impoverished, "when faith in what is good, reverence for what is pure, and relish for what is natural, have died out from a nation's heart."[10]

In the midst of all this ostentatious disillusion, there were few voices besides the "art for art's sake" advocates who dared a reaction against literary moralizing. Occasional objections, though, were made to the didactic novel, few more tellingly than a comment from the Dublin University Magazine in 1860.

> A didactic novel is always an offence against art, and a trial of our good temper. . . . In these days no work of fiction will quite pass muster, unless it hangs out a heavy moral or two at the masthead by way of pacifying the mild religionists, who look on light literature as an overzealous schoolmaster looks upon a half holiday.[11]

There were also extremely rare statements favoring at least one aspect of the new artistic movement--the artist's "instinctive" revolt against middle-class narrowness and the industrial principles of mass production. Writing in the Fortnightly Review in 1865, one author feared the effect of democracy on literature, and spoke of utility versus art:

> . . . the narrow prudence which hates ideas, scorns beauty, and regulates everything with reference to the lowest standard of utility, is quite incompatible with artistic achievement, and . . . it even incapacitates men for comprehending such achievement.[12]

But the general impression created by Victorian periodicals over the issue of religion and art confirms Swinburne's analysis that the society was mostly dominated by a narrow didacticism. It masked desacralization; linked religion, morality, and art, thus allowing a narrowly moral viewpoint to determine popular art; then shaped the opposition to such moralizing in specifically literary directions. Far more than in France, the "art for art's sake" movement in England focused on literary targets, opposing these religious and moral dictates to art rather than generalized bourgeois obtuseness.

Superimposed upon these "godly" concerns were patterns of stability and progress, evidence that the Victorian world could also accommodate Faust--retaining, for example, enough Enlightenment elements to justify progress, enough Romantic belief in human possibility to allow control of the machine. In the midst of revolutionary nineteenth-century Europe, England remained remarkably stable.[13] The working classes were successfully incorporated into the national consensus, the franchise progressively extended, and no Bonaparte threatened. Even with the Industrial Revolution, there were not the historical shocks during the nineteenth century on the scale experienced by France.

Much of the stability and prosperity of Victorian England was attributed by the Victorians themselves to their preeminence in commerce. They measured national greatness in terms of it, and often praised commerce for creating the middle class, though there is some ambivalence in their periodical literature about this group. The middle class was alternately seen as a bastion of stability or as a leveling influence for the entire society, resulting in the democratizing, and hence the mediocrity, of art.[14] These ambivalent attitudes did not extend to commerce. The Victorians went to elaborate lengths to justify their wealth, claiming, for example, as an 1851 article in Fraser's Magazine did, that gold was an "instrument of mercy" when put to "legitimate uses" for wages or education, and that everyone had a duty "to promote the accumulation of wealth, not as an object of worship, but as a minister of good."[15] Nor did Victorian ambivalence extend to their own possible faults. Consciousness of flaws in society was seen positively to place fate squarely in the hands of the Victorians. The catalog of "vice" included the speed and pressure of life, lack of leisure, scant interest in moral theories or good conversation, drunkenness, gambling, blasphemy, though always noting that the last three had begun to disappear.[16]

The optimism inherent in the notion of social improvement which much of this presupposed was underpinned by the idea of progress, especially potent in its Victorian reincarnation because of the coupling, for most people of moral and technological progress. With gradual improvement of social conditions and the zeal for social reform which characterized the period, education became more widespread. John Stuart Mill (though he also feared the pressures of social coercion) elucidated how progressive dissemination of education and enlightenment would make the society increasingly fit for liberty.[17] As if in proof of this imminent occurrence, one author wrote in 1856 that most political questions had been settled. Most wars seemed unlikely in the future, and he found little strife or violence in society, "unless it be among the victims of intemperance."[18] Free trade was like a "healing faith." Any faults in the society were attributed less to depravity than to acquisitiveness, somehow made to seem the least culpable of all offenses.[19] As early as 1820, some English authors spoke of the inevitable perfection of humanity, continuing in this vein until the very end of the century, and often in terms uncannily reminiscent of the St.-Simonians. They supposed that education of the poor would ensure human improvement, and that consistent advances in virtue, moral and intellectual energy, guaranteed the course of the human race toward perfection.[20] Herbert Spencer capsulized much of this thought in his 1851 work, Social Statics. Because Spencer thought evil arose only from lack of congruity between human faculties and their spheres of action, its disappearance was inevitable as people became more highly civilized and thus better adapted to external conditions. Progress implied perfectibility.

> . . . the belief in human perfectibility, merely amounts to the belief, that in virtue of this process, man will eventually become completely suited to his mode of life.
>
> All imperfection is unfitness to the conditions of existence.[21]

The same view of progress and perfectibility as necessary and inevitable permeated Winwood Reade's curious 1872 work, The Martyrdom of Man. The author further asserted that in the future earthly paradise, interest in politics would be transferred to science, and the fine arts would supplant religion. Then in terms which sound like a French creator of utopia, he claimed:

> Not only will Man subdue the forces of evil that are without; he will also subdue those . . . within. . . . The whole world will be united by the same sentiment, which united the primeval clan, and which made its members think, feel, and act as one.[22]

As late as 1901 an article in the Edinburgh Review maintained that "social evolution" focused on moral perfection was the height of human development.[23]

Many of these paeans to progress of the late nineteenth century reflect increasing interest in applying Darwin's ideas to society, including art and literature. A vague social Darwinism was used as a defense against "art for art's sake," perhaps surpassed in foolishness only by applications of the theory to dress.[24] Intended to illustrate Darwinism's "infinite ramifications," the latter showed only how close are the borders of nonsense. As for "art for art's sake," not only was that doctrine thought to be severed from social faith and therefore sterile, but the future here too favored "survival of the fittest." Darwinism aside, some Victorians thought the idea of progress had become so much a part of their society that, in tandem with ethical concerns, it had become the great inspiring force behind literature.[25]

If progress thus conceived helped set intellectual parameters for the society, it derived material support from the observable prosperity of Victorian England. The ethic of individual hard work, in turn, seemed to foster prosperity. Although there are scattered expressions of concern that the individual can become an idol and the standard of achievement, this is not the usual worry in Victorian popular literature. The most famous of all books which took success and hard work for their theme, and thus reinforced this aspect of progress, is Samuel Smiles' Self-Help. First published in 1859, the work went through many editions and graphically illustrates the serious side of the Victorian approach to life. Smiles maintains that steady application to work is the healthiest training for the individual--and for the state as well. Force of purpose, will, education in the "school of Difficulty" are enshrined in Smiles' innumerable examples of successful people.[26] A partial directory of what the "art for art's sake" figures opposed appears early in the book:

> For all experience serves to illustrate and enforce the lesson, that a man perfects himself by work more than by reading--that it is life rather than literature, action rather than study . . . which tend perpetually to renovate mankind.[27]

But we need not rely simply upon Samuel Smiles for documentation of the Victorian passion for work. Cornhill Magazine ran two companion pieces on "work" and "success" in 1860 which illustrated many of these same attitudes. Without work, people were invariably considered unhappy and discontented, a burden to themselves as well as to society. Work was seen as the basis of "all daily blessings"; everything else in life, even the affections, should be cultivated as a means to working well, for nothing else in life seemed quite so ennobling or exhilarating. Even failures could eventually contribute to a success measurable ultimately by what was tried.[28]

A further intellectual foundation for all this lay in the idea of utility. Just as God had supposedly approved work, commerce, and the Victorian definition of progress, He also approved England's "practical utility" as an industrial nation. The only real knowledge was often considered (precisely in those words) what could be useful.

> In an industrial country like this, the practical utility of any study must needs be always thrown into the scale. . . .
>
> Do you not see, then, that by following these studies [scientific] you are walking in the very path to which England owes her wealth; . . . training in yourselves that habit of mind which God has approved as the one which He has ordained for Englishmen.[29]

Literature, too, had its work, and hence its utility. An 1887 work revealingly subtitled A Survey of 50 Years of Progress asserted that poetry and fiction were intended to apply to the problems of human existence, to meld delight with utility, and specifically in the case of the novel, to function as an agent of social improvement.[30] Even recreational literature had the added dimension of making the reader more fit for work.

The undisputed technological progress of Victorian England was thus underpinned by a philosophy of moral progress which drew its sources from utilitarianism and evangelical zeal for social reform. This basic optimism is reflected further in the fact that Victorian periodical literature generally does not show as great a sense of cultural crisis, either real or impending, as French periodicals of the same period. There is considerable interest in religion and morality; articles on "national duty" and "the final triumph of good," for example, are neither surprising nor isolated examples. But the literature is also notable for what is not discussed. Victorian periodicals in general portray a rather self-satisfied society.

The resultant complacency (almost a social narcissism) also meant that there was not the interest in alternative worlds, either utopian or artistic, which existed in France. In spite of Owenite influence on workers' education and organization, their ideal societies never had the exalted character of the French models. Although utopia had not been achieved, neither was it perceived as an alternative to an unintelligible reality.

Unlike mid-nineteenth-century France, the Victorian reality did not seem to be so cluttered as to leave no room for meaning, in Brombert's memorable phrase.[31] Reality was assimilated for the vast majority of Victorians into an ethos of religion, stability, and progress. Unquestionably, Victorian England was more stable than any other major European society of the mid-nineteenth century. Its technological progress was indisputable, and most Victorians chose to apply progress to the moral realm as well. There was general and explicit agreement on the value of stability and progress, reflected in the periodical literature; and whether we look at the Tractarians, the evangelicals, or the noisy debate over science and religion, it is also evident that Victorian England was a society permeated with religious interests, and consciously so.

The implications for the coexistence of God and Faust are enormous. Belief in progress and the obvious stability of the society meant that Faustian possibilities endured. Far more than in France, it still seemed possible to strive for an increasingly rational world implying expanded opportunities for personal achievement, progressive control over nature and human life, and needing neither antidote to remedy ill-fated progress nor theodicy to explain evil and limitation. Progress was a worthy social goal, and evil recognizably different from good--in any event, not a permanent condition. The religious interests of the society meant that God was not merely a passive observer, but a participant in this development. Work, success, and prosperity were all considered godlike and, as we have seen, a case was made for God's will being fulfilled by English wealth. Even though decadence and anxiety were to some extent involved in late Victorian attitudes, both God and Faust could still be conceived in the terms which progress seemed to demand.

In this atmosphere, the artistic responses to desacralization were different from those of the French artists we have examined. Baudelaire, Flaubert, and Gautier all had this, among many other things, in common--that their world was dark and limited, disenchanted, unintelligible except through art. For Walter Pater, on the other hand, reality was not desacralized. The present could be improved, fragmentation overcome, and tradition embraced. The peak moments, even from a spectator's stance, represented a belief in possibility, and in this sense a parallel between the artist and his culture which we have not found in the French anti-Fausts. For A. C. Swinburne, who spanned both French and English artistic traditions, the world ought to be desacralized if it was not, the evil old gods banished, and art made their substitute. When this had been done, human beings could once again control their own destiny. These English advocates of "art for art's sake" thus reacted differently (from the French and from each other) to the cultural crisis of desacralization, sharing to varying degrees in a society whose mythology continued to permit the survival of both God and Faust. Their artistic solutions inevitably reflect their sense of that society and images of that survival.

Notes to Chapter VI

[1]Arthur Tilley, "The Poetic Imagination," Macmillan's Magazine 53 (January 1886):192.

[2]Frances Power Cobbe, "The Morals of Literature," Fraser's Magazine 70 (July 1864):130. Also see "The Office of Literature" (anon.), Macmillan's Magazine53 (March 1886): 362.

[3]Rev. John J. à Becket, "Religious Feeling in Art," The Month 56 (January 1886): 49. Herbert Spencer, Social Statics, or The Conditions Essential to Human Happiness (New York, 1969), p. v: " . . . as it is the purpose of a book to influence conduct, the best way of writing a book must be the way best fitted to effect this purpose."

[4]For one of the best examples, see à Becket, "Religious Feeling in Art."

[5]Quotes taken from "The Moral Element in Literature" (anon.), Cornhill Magazine 43 (January 1881): 43. Also see "Art and Morality" (anon.), Westminster Review 35 (January 1869): 179, 183; "Art and Morality"(anon.), Cornhill Magazine 32 (July 1875): 101. For an especially perceptive article on Ruskin, see J. Milsand, "Une nouvelle théorie de l'art en Angleterre: M. John Ruskin," Revue des deux mondes 4 (30 juin 1860): 184-213.

[6]For the most famous of these attacks, see Thomas Maitland's article on D. G. Rossetti, "The Fleshly School of Poetry," Contemporary Review 18 (October 1871): 334-350. Swinburne and others blamed the viciousness of this article for the beginning of Rossetti's decline.

[7]J. Herbert Stack, "Some Recent English Novels," Fortnightly Review 9 (June 1871): 736. The French agreed about English novels: see Louis Etienne, "Le paganisme poétique en Angleterre," Revue des deux mondes 3 (14 mai 1867): 310.

[8]Quotes from J. G. Wenham, "Poisonous Literature and Its Antidotes," The Month 65 (February 1889): 204. Also see "The Popular Novels of the Year" (anon.), Fraser's Magazine 68 (August 1863): 253-269.

[9]"French Novels" (anon.), Quarterly Review 56 (April 1836): 65 f., 106.

[10]W. R. Greg, "French Fiction: The Lowest Deep," in Literary and Social Judgments, 2 vols. (London, 1877), I, 230. Also see "Art and Morality" (anon.), Westminster Review 35 (January 1869): 181; Frederic W. H. Myers, "The Disenchantment of France," Nineteenth Century 23 (May 1888): 664.

[11]"The Vice of Our Current Literature" (anon.), Dublin University Magazine 56 (November 1860): 520.

[12]Philip Gilbert Hamerton, "The Artistic Spirit," Fortnightly Review 1 (June 15, 1865): 334; also see pp. 333 and 339.

[13]Out of the vast literature on this subject, the following are especially noteworthy: E. J. Hobsbawm, The Age of Revolution 1789-1848 (New York, 1962); E. J. Hobsbawm, Labouring Men: Studies in the History of Labour (New York, 1964); Barrington Moore, Jr., Social Origins of Dictatorship and Democracy (Boston, 1966); Lawrence Stone, Social Change and Revolution in England 1540-1640 (London, 1965); Elie Halévy, The Liberal Awakening 1815-1830 (New York, 1961); E. P. Thompson, The Making of the English Working Class (New York, 1963); R. F. Wearmouth, Methodism and the Working Class Movements of England 1800-1850 (London, 1937); Trygve R. Tholfsen, Working Class Radicalism in Mid-Victorian England (New York, 1977).

[14]"The Decline of Art" Royal Academy and Grosvenor Gallery (anon.), Blackwood's Edinburgh Magazine 138 (July, 1885):4, 25. Also see "What Has Become of the Middle Classes" (anon.), Blackwood's Edinburgh Magazine 138 (August, 1885):174, 177; "The First Half of the Nineteenth Century"(anon.), Fraser's Magazine43 (January, 1851): 4. For a French view, see Nisard, "Les classes moyennes en Angleterre et la bourgeoisie en France," Revue des deux mondes 4 (octobre-novembre-décembre 1849): 968-997.

[15]"The First Half of the Nineteenth Century," Fraser's Magazine (January, 1851): 13, 15.

[16]W. R. Greg, "Life at High Pressure" (1875), in Literary and Social Judgments, II, 263; "The Nineteenth Century" (anon.), Fraser's Magazine 69 (April, 1864):482, 486 f.; "Characteristics in the Nineteenth Century" (anon.), Fraser's Magazine 21 (February, 1840): 156, 161.

[17]John Stuart Mill, Utilitarianism, ed. Oskar Piest (New York, 1957), pp. 20, 41.

[18]John Wade, England's Greatness: Its Rise and Progress in Government, Laws, Religion and Social Life; Agriculture, Commerce, and Manufactures; Science, Literature, and the Arts, from the Earliest Period to the Peace of Paris (London, 1856); quote is on p. 787. Also see pp. 778 f., 783 f.

[19]Ibid., pp. 708, 791. "Our offences are commercial, like our pursuits; they are not crimes of revenge, jealousy, lust, or mere atrocity; but forgery, coining, cheating, fraudulent insolvencies, and joint-stock speculations on public gullibility. Our crimes indicate less of depravity than of a culpable mode of acquiring those objects which are in general request, and form staple social distinctions" (p. 791).

[20]"Wallace's Prospects of Mankind, Nature, and Providence; and on the Progress of Literature" (anon.), Retrospective Review 2 (1820): 192-206.

[21]Spencer, Social statics, quotes on pp. 63 and 64. Also see pp. 59 ff.

[22]Winwood Reade, The Martyrdom of Man (London, 1872), pp. 514 f.

[23]"The Time-spirit of the Nineteenth Century" (anon.), Edinburgh Review 184 (July, 1901): 125 f.

[24]George H. Darwin, "Development in Dress," Macmillan's Magazine 26 (Sepetember, 1872):410-416.

[25]Edward Dowden, Studies in Literature 1789-1877 (London, 1878), p. 111. For an example of "survival of the fittest" applied to literature, see F. T. Palgrave, "The Decline of Art," Nineteenth Century 23 (January, 1888): 71-92.

[26]Samuel Smiles, Self-help (London, 1958). For Smiles' explicit statements, rather than examples only, see pp. 58, 228 ff., 325.

[27]Ibid., p. 39.

[28]"Work" (anon.), Cornhill Magazine 2 (November, 1860): 599, 602, 607 f.; "Success" (anon.), Cornhill Magazine 2 (December, 1860): 729-741.

[29]Charles Kingsley, "How to Study Natural History" (1846), in Scientific Lectures and Essays (London, 1899), pp. 289-310, 305, 308. For a classic statement on useful knowledge, see J. A. Froude, "On Progress," in Short Studies on Great Subjects, ed. David Ogg (London, 1963), pp. 293 f.; "The knowledge which a man can use is the only real knowledge, the only knowledge which has life and growth in it, and converts itself into practical power."

[30]Thomas Humphrey Ward, ed., The Reign of Queen Victoria: A Survey of 50 Years of Progress, 2 vols. (London, 1887), II, 445 ff., 493.

[31]Victor Brombert, The Novels of Flaubert (Princeton, 1966), p. 285.

CHAPTER VII

WALTER PATER AND THE SELF

Of all of the "art for art's sake" figures in Victorian England, Walter Pater is the most paradoxical. A hidden man, unknown to most of his contemporaries and virtually unknowable to us today because his work reveals so little of the self behind the writer's mask, he influenced an entire generation of young men at Oxford. A master of prose, he gave up poetry in early life, fortunately for his later literary reputation. An avowed classicist, he was among the first to speak of the ills of modernity and probably would have been equally uncomfortable in any age. And within the context of "art for art's sake" he pushed one aspect of this doctrine to its furthest possible extension. According to Pater, life itself should be lived in the spirit of art--a mirror image of the old Aristotelean dictum (newly revived by Ruskin) that art imitates nature. With Pater, art becomes the model for life. Yet Pater himself always remained the spectator, much too removed from life's realities to create believable fictional characters in his few tries at this genre, and beneath the urgings toward passionate experience of each moment, we meet the bland and calm face of the observer of both art and life for whom passion was perhaps a stranger or infrequent guest. What Walter Pater was not seems so overwhelming that it is often difficult to measure what he was.

Pater remains unapproachable merely as the disguised humanist secretly interested in religion or as the artist explainable by temperament alone. To apply religious categories to Pater is deceptively easy, probably because of the increasingly religious tone of his interests in later years. But viewed from the perspective of his lifetime, Pater was not a religious figure and his artistic theories begin and culminate in a doctrine of "art for art's sake." He becomes much more intelligible, even as an apostle of "culture," as a re-shaper of the "l'art pour l'art" tradition within a society in which a Faustian artistic response to the problem of desacralization was more possible than in France. Beneath the layers of mystery, Pater made a distinctly Victorian contribution to the meaning of "art for art's sake."

From the fairly small body of his work, the most immediately striking fact is that Romantic striving is reaffirmed, though always from a spectator's position, along with his own version of Enlightenment rationalism. Contrary to Baudelaire's and Flaubert's anti-Faustian posture and Gautier's re-enchanter, Pater reaffirms both sides of the old dialectic. Basically, the problem of desacralization is different for Pater. Art becomes an antidote to fragmentation, loss of self, bestiality, and assorted symptomatic ills of the modern age, not to possible causes of these. Nor does he deal with questions of limitation and evil. In his societal dimension, Pater is linked to Victorian experiences of stability and religiosity. In his world, man can still be Faust. Because reality is not irrevocably desacralized, a return to tradition, even a flirtation with Christianity, is both possible and desirable. The peak moments of the Romantic striver can still provide reason for life and art, and for us a key to Pater's thought.

Pater's classic statement of the peak moment is contained in his Studies in the History of the Renaissance, a period that for him held a charm second only to classical Greece.

> How can we pass most swiftly from point to point, and be present always at the focus where the greatest number of vital forces unite in their purest energy? To burn always with this hard gem-like flame, to maintain this ecstasy, is success in life.[1]

"This ecstasy" is a multifaceted idea. In his essay on Wordsworth, Pater notes the poet's interest in the speech of rural people, then tells us something about himself when he distinguishes the language of ordinary intercourse from that of "certain select moments of vivid sensation."[2] The only one of his fictional characters who emerges even with half-success, Marius the Epicurean, seeks to live so completely in these moments of distinction that the other, ordinary times, "the mere drift and debris of life," become virtually nonexistent. Improvement of the present moment, the only real moment, is Marius' aim--through training his own capacities, to enter a world of "realized consciousness."[3]

This consciousness of the peak moment is applied directly to the artistic process in one of Pater's studies of Plato. Pater distinguishes full consciousness in the process of making art, opposed to a random quality which can either become incoherent or fall to pieces.[4] It is this same quality which he translates to life itself in the ending to a fairly early essay on William Morris which later became the famous conclusion to his Renaissance studies:

> . . . we have an interval, and then our place knows us no more. Some spend this interval in listlessness, some in high passions, the wisest in art and song. For our one chance is in expanding that interval, in getting as many pulsations as possible into the given time. High passions give one this quickened sense of life, ecstasy and sorrow of love, political or religious enthusiasm, or the 'enthusiasm of humanity.' Only, be sure it is passion, that it does yield you this fruit of a quickened, multiplied consciousness. Of this wisdom, the poetic passion, the desire of beauty, the love of art for art's sake has most; for art comes to you professing frankly to give nothing but the highest quality to your moments as they pass, and simply for those moments' sake.[5]

All that Pater believes of consciousness is condensed here. The ecstatic moments in art and life are identical, but there is no question which produces the other.

Pater sums up this blend of Romantic yearning for the impossible in one of his imaginary portraits: "He was always a seeker after something in the world that [exists] in no satisfying measure, or not at all."[6] When we consider that Pater wrote this in Victorian England, not in the age of Coleridge and Wordsworth, it seems possible that some kind of Romantic yearning may have lain close to the core of Pater's work and personality. Hough places Pater among his "last romantics" who "visited history" not as earlier Romantics, "spectators, intelligent tourists," but "as exiles from a lost paradise."[7] Certainly there is ample evidence of traditional Romantic themes and longing in Pater's "The Chant of the Celestial Sailors" published posthumously.

Homeward! homeward! gentle brothers,
    to the tranquil morning land.

. . . .

Now, behold the crystal morning
    Paves the East with rosy dyes;
All the hues of heavenly dawning
    Rise to our expectant eyes.[8]

Though almost certainly Pater never intended this to be printed, the Romantic themes in it are undeniable. There is some ambivalence in Pater, however, about the meanings of Romanticism. He once defined the "Romantic type" as representing "that inexhaustible discontent, languor, and home-sickness, the chords of which ring all through our modern literature."[9] But Pater also thinks that "classical" and "romantic" define two real tendencies in the history of art, and that there need not be opposition between them. They are reduced to aspects of beauty in Pater's claim that the romantic character in art is the "addition of strangeness to beauty." This strangeness can range from exertion of artistic charm over us to the fascination of corruption.[10]

Although this may sound somewhat like Baudelaire, Pater does not seem to have known much about the French poet and not his poetry in any case.[11] Pater's chief French influence was Flaubert, though by the late nineteenth century the ideas of "l'art pour l'art" in general were widely known in English literary circles, chiefly through Swinburne's efforts. Like the French figures we have examined, Pater urges that art be pursued for its own sake, but he also finds antecedents for this in Plato, claiming that the Greek thinker anticipated the "modern notion that art as such has no end but its own perfection--art for art's sake."[12] Yet, however often Pater repeats this, we cannot avoid the impression that his real interest is in "art for self's sake." Art teaches life, patterns it, and mirrors it.

Pater's statements of the peak moment and reliance on instinct, which will be unerring and good, constitute his personal version of Romanticism, however misplaced its historical chronology. There is another early Romantic anachronism here also in the unspoken assumption that peak moments can be created, that human beings can make such times for themselves if only they will train their sensibilities. In this sense, Romantic yearning need not go perpetually unfulfilled. But the peak moments are also reminiscent of Flaubert's never-satisfied St. Antoine, who, when he has finally experienced all there is to know of world, time, and the gods, desires union with matter itself. Typical of much of his thought, Pater's Romanticism is ambivalent.

In its social dimension, Pater's idea of the peak moments implies opposition to the work doctrine and moral earnestness of Victorian England, which as Houghton notes meant that the writer, like everyone else in the society, had work to do. He was not free to live a life of aesthetic pleasure.[13] For Pater this is hardly a question. Art is life itself, and both art and life center not on work or morality, but on the peak moments. This idea has many other dimensions as well. Pater was always intensely interested (it might have approached fanaticism in anyone else) in the self and the personal in art. One of his essays defines an artist as one who transcribes not the world or mere fact, but his sense of it. In an article on Flaubert, Pater praises the French master's precision of language, but then argues that ascertaining one's own meaning is the prerequisite to saying to the reader, "I want you to see precisely what I see."[14] Although Flaubert's theories of art continued to interest Pater throughout his life, he parts company with him here. The personal is the beginning, end, and focal point for Pater, and because the writer's or artist's subjectivity selects and colors all he does, Pater thinks that impersonality in art is impossible. In aesthetic study of any kind, "the salt . . . is in the question--what, precisely what, is this to me?"[15] For anyone, knowledge of an object begins with knowledge of one's own impression. For the working artist, personal quality seals his work and makes imaginative works themselves worth having.[16]

The personal thus becomes a guide to artistic truth and criticism; it can also lead to under-standing everything else through understanding the self--a type of new Hellas which always remained Pater's ideal,[17] and another striking example of the congruence he found between life and art. Yet at least once Pater seemed to doubt even the possibility of understanding.

> Experience, already reduced to a swarm of impressions, is ringed round for each one of us by that thick wall of personality through which no real voice has ever pierced on its way to us, or from us to that which we can only conjecture to be without. Every one of those impressions is the impression of an individual in his isolation, each mind keeping as a solitary prisoner its own dream of a world.[18]

That self is the center and that the world may be illusion, are clearly stated here. But we are left with the puzzle of whether or not understanding can ever really embrace either self or world. Pater's ideas on contemplation provide clarification. The key to any kind of understanding which may exist lies in contemplation, an idea central to Pater's thought. Pater claims that if men needed lessons, this should be the first: contemplation is the purpose of life. The true moral significance of art is to make possible life treated in the spirit of art, withdrawn briefly from the "machinery of life" and fixed upon the spectacle of human grandeur and suffering.[19] We understand life, self and art through contemplation, but art remains the catalyst.

Art has many other purposes for Pater besides providing the key to understanding self and world. Literature can be a refuge from vulgarity, enlarging the person when it contains "something of the soul of humanity."[20] In one of his letters, Pater refers specifically to art's purpose to help people "forget the crude and the violent,"[21] a kind of moral purpose not always shared by many of Pater's more narrow and didactic Victorian contemporaries. Art is essential to culture and rooted in it. Like Baudelaire, Pater thinks that art must be historically grounded, following and catching the spirit of its own time. But, like Flaubert, he also urges art's transcendent qualities. Flaubert conceived transcendence in abstract truth, independent of time and place. For Pater, the transcendent standard is the production of genius of past ages against which the artist can measure his own works.[22]

In the most self-revelatory of his works, "The Child in the House,"[23] Pater shows other aspects of his artistic theory. The work is filled with a sensual love of matter, somewhat like Flaubert's St. Antoine; the nostalgia for childhood of the uprooted adult; and a passionate, almost overripe quality reminiscent of Baudelaire. "The Child in the House" shows also, better even than Pater's essays, the practice of his own meticulous tenets on style. Above all, Pater values control. In one of his essays on Plato, Pater opposes the spirit of artistic control to the general course of life, its energy and passion. Like the other devotees of "art for art's sake," he maintains that control generates form, and that form is everything.[24] Like Flaubert, Pater attaches crucial importance to the precise word, literary success itself being based on saying exactly what the author wills. Pater's idea of the original unity of the artistic vision is also similar to Flaubert's idea that clear thought leads the words onto the page. Then, like Baudelaire, Pater emphasizes the receiver. Although he also maintains after all this that artistic success cannot be strictly analyzed, Pater finds the reader's intuition always significant.[25] Style, however, not congruence between author and reader, is the final unifying principle in art, just as art itself unites world and self.

Pater has much to say about unity, to the point that the "spiritual unity" of the world involves the "congruity of all things with one another," even the teacher's personality with what is taught and the manner of expression.[26] And for Pater's alter ego, Marius, a world filled with sacred presences seems to require "a similar collectedness" from himself.[27] This, too, is a version of the peak moments which demand a focusing and totality of human energy. In one of his more poetic passages from "The Child in the House," Pater conjures an almost cosmic, pantheistic unity:" . . . irresistibly, little shapes, voices, accidents--the angle at which the sun in the morning fell on the pillow--become part of the great chain wherewith we are bound."[28]

Art points toward unity, and unity produces culture. What Pater means by "culture" is very clear. He distinguishes two impulses or ideals in the moral life of mankind, the Ascetic and the Cultural.[29] The Ascetic sacrifices one part of human nature to the perfection of the whole nature. Culture aims at harmonious development of all the parts of human nature, proportioned to each other, and existing fully in that refined sensation of the hard, gemlike flame. The final perfection of culture is peace.[30] All these thoughts point to a man for whom the world had a center. Life's disparities could be unified and understood in art and culture. If not strictly speaking perfectible, humanity could be, after all, redeemed.

Numerous passages in Pater's works testify to his basically optimistic view of human nature. The doctrine of peak moments and the idea that life ought to be lived in the spirit of art underline emphatically his position that a human being can seize the moment and make of it a work of art. There are even some curious passages in which Pater seems to invoke barely disguised notions of progress and perfectibility, though unlike the French utopians always with the emphasis on being as opposed to doing. His fictional character Marius describes the author's position best.

> Revelation, vision, the uncovering of a vision, the _seeing_ of a perfect humanity, in a perfect world--through all his alterations of mind, by some dominant instinct determined by the original necessities of his own nature and character, he had always set that above the _having_, or even the _doing_, of anything. [Such vision was] . . . in reality, the _being_ something. . . .[31]

The artist and the person who has treated life in the spirit of art desires finally to confront the world as he really is. Although Pater has difficulty being specific about this transparent nature, he does seem to equate it with the hard gemlike flame, his ideal of humanity. He states flatly that a majority like this in society would regenerate the world. That Pater realizes the impossibility of his ideal is evident from his brief considerations of "spiritual progress" confined to a few.[32] Perhaps the attraction of the ideal would be dimmed, even on an individual level, if it were too readily realizable. On the level of society, there is also the historical moment to be considered. Gaston de Latour describes the early days of the Renaissance poised between an old ideal which still haunted humanity at the moment when "it [humanity] was called, through a full knowledge of the past, to enjoy the present with an unrestricted expansion of its own capacities."[33] We are left with the inescapable impression from Pater's work that individually and collectively the focusing of human energies will always remain an impossible ideal.

But if this better person is ultimtely an illusion, the quest for him, for one's own nature fully actualized, preserves the individual from the even greater illusion of external reality. Such redemption as exists lies in the self. The key to what Marius saw as "improvement of the present" lies in self-improvement. The underlying assumption takes a page from Enlightenment theory--that human freedom and possibility (in this case, to create the self) are virtually infinite. When the artistic, cultured self has been thus created, humanity can be seen in a new way and the common world replaced with a better and happier creation.[34] Pater is closer to Gautier than to either Baudelaire or Flaubert in his emphasis on the alternative world created through art. But his chief interest always remains the alternative self made possible through art.

For all his interest in the self, perhaps because of it, Pater has a keen appreciation of modernity. It is possible from his works to reconstruct his portrait of an age and the individual's relation to it. Pater finds Victorian times transitional, but not in the sense of much Victorian periodical literature. He thinks the nineteenth century is still linked to the Renaissance when human potentialities seemed infinite. But his age of transition has not yet seen the birth of anything new, in spite of obvious technological and scientific progress, and he compares the color of modern culture unfavorably with the heat and profundity of Medieval culture and the light of Hellenism.[35] In his essay on Coleridge, Pater sketches other elements of modern life, its "inexhaustible discontent, languor and home-sickness, that endless regret," all of which (as we have seen) he allies to the Romantic impulse in literature. Distinguishing Coleridge's "passion for the absolute," Pater finds fluidity central to modern life.[36] In the face of constant flux, the individual asserts his freedom to make of his life a work of art. This sense of freedom is for Pater the greatest spiritual need of the modern world. In turn, individual freedom produces that selfhood which Pater calls completeness, centrality. He thinks unity with self is far harder to achieve in the modern world than in ancient Greece.[37] But the ideal remains the same. The sorrows, preoccupations and bewilderment of modern experience must be integrated if the spirit is to survive. Art, which teaches life and leads to life, performs this integrating function.

We have seen in Pater's theories of art his emphasis on the personal to the extent that art can create the self; the importance of contemplation ("being" opposed to "doing"); art as refuge and truth; art's unifying function for the person and the culture; and, finally, his views on the modern world. All these diverse elements converge in the larger question of what art explains for Pater. Because the world is an illusion for him, more than any of the other "art for art's sake" figures we have examined Pater finds a sharp dichotomy between the exterior and the interior worlds. Art teaches life, in his view, but it is the interior life of the spirit, a highly individualized and detached existence. Pater states flatly, and the point has been underlined by a recent commentator, that because the world is an illusion, disengagement is essential.[38] It seems far more plausible that Pater's real intent is the opposite. Because disengagement is essential, the world is an illusion. To cultivate the self, exterior reality must be considered even more ephemeral than it already is. But there is another way of looking at this. If the world is truly an illusion in that it is fleeting and unknowable except in relation to the self, knowledge of self and detachment from the passing world are equally essential. Cultivation of the self in its own unity and completeness is necessary for detachment but also the fruit of it.

A further question flowing from Pater's work involves how the world is an illusion, and Pater gives two complementary answers to this problem. On the one hand, exterior reality is illusory because it is not the center of human existence. However much Pater sometimes decries the modern emphasis on experience, (". . . the whole scope of observation is dwarfed to the narrow chamber of the individual mind"),[39] his basic focus on the self favors this. Individual experience and the tangle of modern life can be integrated through the self and its perceptions of its own inner workings. The world is an illusion, then, first of all, because self is the true center. On the other hand, exterior reality alone is an illusion because world and self are also somehow indistinguishable. With Pater, we have come round fully to Shattuck's idea of the world revolving around us and indistinguishable from us. Baudelaire's <u>flâneur</u> existed at the point of equilibrium. Pater's identity is far more self-centered in the fullest sense of that term. Art exists primarily for the self, as an antidote to the fragmentation of self and world. Both the necessity of integration and the way of integration are shown through art. This largely explains Pater's overriding interest in the unity of the Greek character, in which he finds sensations, ideas, experiences filtered by and centered in the highly cultivated individual. Art is not merely an antidote to bestiality, sadness, stupidity, and savagery. It is this also, of course, paralleling the French tradition of "l'art pour l'art." But for Pater, art is primarily an antidote to division and fragmentation. It is almost as if he took literally Flaubert's admonition to "make an egoism and live there" during a savage age.

Art's integrating function creates its own kind of illusion. The self seems to be made whole. For Baudelaire, art conjured the evil half of life; for Flaubert, the indispensability of illusion and limitation; and for Gautier art created an alternative world of dream. In Pater's dispensation, art's conjuring of illusion begins and ends with the individual. Even Gautier's dream world existed independent of the person. As observers who expressed the "non-I," the world revolving around the individual, Baudelaire, Flaubert, and Gautier were more truly outside, and thus somehow transcended, their own mere individuality. They spoke with a far more universal voice than Walter Pater. For that reason, they were able to reorder exterior reality. Pater, less connected with the external world, cannot reorder that world. There is no question of evil or the need to justify its part in human existence. Unlike Baudelaire's focus on "life's indispensable sadness," Pater seems to find in art an antidote to sadness. Viewed solely from this angle, his version of "art for art's sake" has no social dimension whatever, and there is certainly a purely egotistical component in Pater's work. If there were only this, he would have little to say beyond his admonitions about style and the proper word. However, in pointing to the self-world fragmentation inherent in modernity, Pater also shows a way out, highly individualistic but not totally so. Fragmentation can be overcome through art and a return to tradition. Pater's artistic theories thus comprise a collective as well as an individual dimension.

For the individual the ecstasy of art, the precise mirroring of intent and will in the creative impulse, leads to the ecstasy of life, the investing of each moment with all that is most precious in the self. Life spent in the spirit of art can only be described as ecstatic, in Pater's lexicon. In opposition to his contemporary, Swinburne, who set art against life, Walter Pater links the two as part of his solution to the fragmentation of self and world. It may be worth noting that his theory hardly bore the weight of practice. With the French advocates of "l'art pour l'art" whom we have examined, practice and theory were more nearly aligned. Baudelaire the _flâneur_ was also Baudelaire the dandy, carrying his pose of insensiblity into action. Flaubert actually did struggle for years in producing each of his beloved "old books," and as clearly as any man lived for his art. Even Gautier carried his artistic ideal of the dream world into his travel literature (the medium of journalism hardly lent itself to much dreaming). But Pater's artistic ideal of life in the spirit of art, lived always at the peak moments, is even further removed from possibility than any of these other ideals. It is probably as impossible for an individual to live thus as for a century to be in constant, unmitigated crisis. Furthermore, Pater's rather bland character, at least as he is knowable to us, forms a decided contrast with his artistic ideal, though the ideal seems not less valid for that. On the individual level, it offers a theoretical solution to the modern fragmentation of self and world, valuable both as a personal ideal and for what it reveals of a latent tendency in "art for art's sake." With Pater, life imitates art.

Fragmentation can also be overcome through a return to tradition, linking the individual to a wider human experience. Pater's historical ideals, the tradition before which he bowed, were classical Greece and the Renaissance because in his mind these were periods of unity. That he saw these times from a somewhat myopic viewpoint, seeing precisely and only what he wished to see, does not alter the force of his ideal. Pater thought the individual should be linked to time and culture, but free to shape his own life in the spirit of art. Since it was impossible to return to Greek and Renaissance times, his solution was to emulate their spirit of unity and culture. There is an anti-progress impulse here as well. Because the peak moments are basically transcendental experiences, art explains to some extent why material progress is unimportant. Though Pater does not deride progress in the manner of the French "l'art pour l'art" advocates, he thinks that modernity impairs freedom. In his essay on Winckelmann, Pater discusses necessity and freedom.

> What modern art has to do in the service of culture is so to rearrange the details of modern life, so to reflect it, that it may satisfy the spirit. And what does the spirit need in the face of modern life? The sense of freedom . . . . penetrating us with a network subtler than our subtlest nerves. Can art represent men and women in these bewildering toils so as to give the spirit at least an equivalent for the sense of freedom?[40]

His "equivalent for the sense of freedom" becomes freedom itself in the peak moments. Interestingly, Pater skips the Enlightenment completely in his cultural diagnosis, undoubtedly because it is too rationalistic for him. His ideal, expressed most fully in his essays on the Renaissance and in the character of Marius, is the blending of sensation and intellect which he purportedly finds only in classical Greece and the Renaissance. Through contact with these periods, his nineteenth-century world is made more amenable to human existence, though never reordered in the mode of the French anti-Fausts. The focus always remains on the self, on individual life as art. But in this limited sense, Pater's reality, too, becomes meaningful again, in a secular way through culture and in a personal way through art.

Pater's artistic theories comprise thus an antidote to the fragmentation of the individual more than to mediocrity and stupidity. The real milieu within which individuality should be considered is its lost contact with culture and time. This contact is what Pater seeks to restore in his version of "art for art's sake." Pater's cultural/personal antidote to fragmentation implies Enlightenment and Romantic possibilities revisited. Pater's world is ruled by culture and individual potential. Because of art, fragmentation (cultural or personal) need not be a permanent condition. Sensation and intellect both have their role in reaffirming what human beings can do and become.

Pater's failure to deal with questions of evil and limitation means that his version of "art for art's sake" does not extend to a theodicy. But, since Pater follows the French "l'art pour l'art" tradition in other ways (and we have seen that some kind of theodicy seems to have been implicit in this), the deeper problem lies in determining what this tradition means in mid-and late-Victorian England.

Pater's theories obviously reflect the influence of Flaubert, at least one volume of whose published correspondence he reviewed for <u>The Anthenaeum</u> in 1889.[41] Pater's review of Flaubert's letters covered those written between 1850 and 1854, precisely the letters which detailed most of Flaubert's theories of art. The "l'art pour l'art" movement itself was known in England chiefly through Swinburne. Pater shares the movement's concern for style, form, precision, strangeness in beauty, art as an ivory tower and refuge from vulgarity. But his interest in personal experience is a distinct departure from "l'art pour l'art" tenets. Although the early Romantics in both France and England had focused on personal experience, it has more immediate roots for Pater. By the time Pater produced most of his work, the Pre-Raphaelite emphasis on fidelity to inner experience and what Hough has called "the attitude of the cloistered and devoted aesthete" were well known in English artistic circles. Though it is impossible to trace direct influence (Pater remains a hidden figure here, too), his roots may also lie to some extent in this English tradition.[42] Certainly both Pre-Raphaelite and "l'art pour l'art" attitudes were readily available to English artistic figures. But Pater is linked to Victorian England in a still more significant way.

His was a society largely dominated, as we have seen, by interests in utility and progress, and by a religiosity and morality which muted the problem of desacralization. There had been no nineteenth-century shocks in England on the French model. In some sense, therefore, man could still be Faust, and a return to tradition, even in its Christian dimensions, was both possible and desirable. In his later years, Pater showed considerable interest in religion, and, unlike the French anti-Fausts, found a role for it in society. In one of his essays for the Guardian, he writes that " . . . men's horizons are enlarged by religion."[43] During the outwardly religious period of his later life, Pater even wonders if religion is not "the only way in which poetry can really reach the hard-worked poor."[44]

If the Faustian possibilities still inherent in Victorian England thus allowed a return to tradition, they also supported Pater's version of Romantic striving in his theory of the peak moments. The peaks themselves were still possible in a society which prided itself on technology and utility and which had not yet discovered to the extent France had how great were the ruins of the Christian ethos. It is difficult to imagine Baudelaire and Flaubert, immersed as they were in human impossibility rather than its opposite, writing of peak moments.

Walter Pater thus stands a little to the side of the tradition of "l'art pour l'art." Unquestionably, he shared much of it, as we have seen, and expressed it as eloquently as any:

> Of this wisdom, the poetic passion, the desire of beauty, the love of art for art's sake has most; for art comes to you professing frankly to give nothing but the highest quality to your moments as they pass, and simply for those moments' sake.[45]

But Pater was essentially a re-shaper of a French tradition filtered through Flaubert and the other "l'art pour l'art" advocates and perhaps heavily dosed with Pre-Raphaelite personalism. Where Pater appropriated this artistic tradition as his own is his emphasis on the peak moments, the quest for one's own nature fully actualized. There are two implicit reversals here: the area of Faustian possibility becomes wholly internal, and life becomes the imitator of art. In this latter sense, Pater pushed a latent aspect of the "l'art pour l'art" doctrine to its furthest extent. In the end, however, because of his ties with his own society, because he was a Victorian and could still believe in human possibility, Walter Pater was incapable of approaching the desacralized bedrock upon which "l'art pour l'art" rested. A. C. Swinburne was closer to the French tradition and, by that very fact, more removed from Victorian England.

Notes to Chapter VII

[1]Walter H. Pater, Studies in the History of the Renaissance (London, 1873), p. 210.

[2]Walter Pater, Essays from 'The Guardian' (London, 1901), p. 102.

[3]Walter Pater, Marius the Epicurean: His Sensations and Ideas, 2 vols. (London, 1885), I, 57, 160.

[4]Walter Pater, Plato and Platonism (London, 1893), p. 252.

[5]Pater, Studies in the History of the Renaissance, pp. 212 f.

[6]Walter Pater, "A Prince of Court Painters," in Imaginary Portraits by Walter Pater: A New Collection, ed. Eugene J. Brzenk (New York, 1964), p. 113.

[7]Hough, The Last Romantics, pp. xiv f.

[8]Walter Pater, "The Chant of the Celestial Sailors," an unpublished poem, 30cc., printed by E. H. Blakeney at his private press, 1928.

[9]Walter Pater, "Coleridge's Writings," Westminster Review 29 (January 1866): 132.

[10]Walter Pater, Appreciations (London, 1915), p. 246. Also see Studies in the History of the Renaissance, pp. 62, 98.

[11]Enid Starkie, From Gautier to Eliot: The Influence of France on English Literature 1851-1939 (London, 1960), p. 52.

[12]Pater, Plato and Platonism, pp. 244 f., 252. Also see Appreciations, p. 109.

[13]Walter E. Houghton, The Victorian Frame of Mind, (London, 1957), pp. 265, 117.

[14]Pater, Appreciations, p. 31. Also see pp. 9 f.

[15]Walter Pater, "Notre-Dame d'Amiens," Miscellaneous Studies (London, 1899), p. 98. Also see Walter Pater, "Correspondance de Gustave Flaubert, 1850-54," Anthenaeum, no. 3223 (3 August 1889), p. 155.

[16]Pater, Studies in the History of the Renaissance, pp. viii, 60 f.

[17]Walter Pater, "Duke Carl of Rosenmold," Imaginary Portraits by Walter Pater, ed. Brzenk, p. 158. Also see Walter Pater, Greek Studies (London, 1895).

[18]Walter Pater, "Poems by William Morris," Westminster Review 34 (October 1868): 310 f.

[19]Pater, Appreciations, pp. 62 f., 59.

[20]Ibid., p. 38.

[21]To George Moore [c. 3 August 1887], Letters of Walter Pater, ed. Lawrence Evans (Oxford, 1970), p. 111. Dates given in brackets are those of the editor.

[22]Pater, Studies in the History of the Renaissance, p. 169 f.

[23]Walter Pater, "The Child in the House," Miscellaneous Studies (London, 1899). Also published separately as An Imaginary Portrait (Oxford, 1894).

[24]Pater, Plato and Platonism, pp. 258, 4.

[25]Pater, Appreciations, pp. 22, 33; "Pascal," Miscellaneous Studies, p. 52.

[26]Walter Pater, Gaston de Latour: An Unfinished Romance (London,1896), p. 192.

[27]Pater, Marius the Epicurean, I, 19.

[28]Pater, "The Child in the House," p. 152.

[29]Pater's formulations of culture vs. asceticism are usually cast in pseudo-psychological, ahistorical terms. For a historical study of the

idea of culture, see Raymond Williams, Culture and Society 1780-1950 (New York, 1966). Williams traces the idea of culture to the period of the Industrial Revolution, and "our reactions, in thought and feeling, to the changed conditions of our common life. Our meaning of culture is a response to the events which our meanings of industry and democracy most evidently define" (p. 295).

[30]Pater, Marius the Epicurean, II, 136.

[31]Ibid., pp. 239 f.

[32]Walter Pater, "Diaphanéite," Miscellaneous Studies, pp. 217, 222. Also see Studies in the History of the Renaissance, p. 172.

[33]Pater, Gaston de Latour, p. 103.

[34]Pater, Studies in the History of the Rennaisance, p. 186.

[35]Ibid., p. 160. And see letter to the Pall Mall Gazette, 27 November 1886, Letters of Walter Pater, p. 102. On the same subject, also see Pater, Appreciations, p. 104; Gaston de Latour, p. vi; and Studies in the History of the Renaissance, p. 205.

[36]Walter Pater, "Coleridge's Writings," Westminster Review (January 1866), p. 132.

[37]Pater, Studies in the History of the Renaissance, pp. 201 f.

[38]Pater, "Sebastian Van Storck," pp. 134 f. Also see the introduction by the editor.

[39]Pater, Studies in the History of the Renaissance, p. 209.

[40]Ibid., p. 205.

[41]Pater, "Correspondance de Gustave Flaubert."

[42]For the quote, see Hough, The Last Romantics, p. 67. Regarding Pater's intellectual antecedents in the Pre-Raphaelite Brotherhood, Hough concludes only

that "the ethic of Pater and the immoralism of the nineties might both trace their origin to this source" (p. 53).

[43]Pater, Essays from 'The Guardian,' pp. 56 f.

[44]To Edward Vincent Eyre, 1 July [1893], Letters of Walter Pater, p. 244.

[45]Pater, Studies in the History of the Renaissance, pp. 212 f.

CHAPTER VIII

A. C. SWINBURNE AND THE DEATH OF THE GODS

Algernon Charles Swinburne's version of "art for art's sake" is more highly nuanced, more varied, more modern than Walter Pater's, and more fully developed than that of his French masters. Typical of an unbridled quality in Swinburne's character and work, his theories outdo their French origins. In his hands, "art for art's sake" reaches its most strident expression, combining Gautier's rage against the bourgeoisie with Flaubert's carefully constructed theories of beauty. More solidly in this French mainstream than Pater, Swinburne launches a broadside against his own society and a venomous defense of art's right to exist of and for itself. In giving "l'art pour l'art" a decidedly negative thrust, Swinburne makes what art opposes as important as what art is. The lexicon of opposition includes the familiar targets of utilitarianism, moral purpose, democracy, nature--and, more curiously, life itself and the old gods and myths by which people had lived. Art is for Swinburne a substitute god, life-sustaining and consuming. All this is evident from the poet's theories of art, for although Swinburne is primarily a poet, his life in Victorian England produced not only venom but an elaborate theory to justify his work.

Among the first to recognize the importance of William Blake, Swinburne wrote an essay on that forerunner of Romanticism which serves as a vehicle for his own artistic tenets as much as an introduction to Blake. There is an absolutist quality about Swinburne which appears in this fairly early essay unobscured yet by the sheer ranting of his later letters to editors. Unlike Pater, who supposes that art fosters the ecstatic life, Swinburne deliberately sets life and art in opposition.

> And if to live well be really better than to write or paint well, and a noble action more valuable than the greatest poem or the most perfect picture, let us have done at once with the meaner things that stand in the way of the higher.[1]

His purpose is to strip art of any connection with religion, duty, science, morality--the Victorian gods he constantly decries. All true deities are for Swinburne summed up in art. "Art for art's sake" means unremitting opposition to moral purpose and to what Swinburne always calls "Philistia."

> "Poetry must conform itself to" etc; "art must have a mission and meaning appreciable by serious men in an age of work" and so forth. These be thy gods, O Philistia.[2]

Swinburne pursues the same themes in his 1862 review of Baudelaire's Les fleurs du mal, lamenting that poets are expected to redeem their age or remold society rather than simply to produce good verse.[3] Swinburne does allow for didacticism in prose, however, a practice he himself pursues all his life in his vituperative letters to debtors and cranky fulminations against his critics. The cranky quality as well as the theory are well displayed in Notes on Poems and Reviews.

> It would seem indeed as though to publish a book were equivalent to thrusting it with violence into the hands of every mother and nurse in the kingdom as fit and necessary food for female infancy.[4]

Swinburne thinks the basic issue is whether art must give no offense. If such is the case, poets who contravene the reigning ideas of virtue are naturally considered immoral. With Flaubert, the English poet argues that literature must embrace all of human life, that it must be large and liberal, and adds that it "cannot be chaste if it be prudish."[5] Like Gautier, he excoriates the bourgeois, though unlike the French poet, Swinburne seems to have considered him uneducable. Notes on Poems and Reviews and the work on Blake are filled with denunciations of "Philistia" and "Puritanism"; Swinburne argues that in no past century or in no present nation are poets expected to labor under these difficulties which they face in England.

Whether he is speaking of Victorian prudishness or French social theory, Swinburne's quarrel with his age reduces itself to opposing any god other than art. More than any other devotee of "art for art's sake" in either France or England, Swinburne exalts and separates art from all theories of personal or social morality or progress. He is a "true believer" along the lines he perceives in Blake, and advancing age scarcely blunts, though it does refine somewhat, his sense of art's primacy. The vituperation of the 1860's gradually gives way to the mellowness of the years with Theodore Watts-Dunton,[6] although Swinburne is still capable of writing an occasional scathing letter to one of the periodicals he favors with his scorn.

In the interests of purity in art viewed from another aspect, his opposition is to bad verse, regardless of the subject. Swinburne considers the poet's role simply to produce good verse. Fine poetry can always endure analysis, a concept he explores in Under the Microscope. The test of great poetry is not whether its subject is noble or great, but whether it can be analyzed: "It is not more praiseworthy or more pardonable to write bad verse about . . . gaol-birds than to write bad verse about kings."[7] This is a departure from Pater's stance (and that of the Romantics) that great poetry has something of the soul of humanity in it, and more aligned to Gautier's interest in writing poetry about a hand, a radish, or a red dress, but hardly unexpected in Swinburne, who follows the French tradition of "l'art pour l'art" much more closely than Pater.

The Pre-Raphaelite Brotherhood was also perhaps influential in some of these poetic attitudes. Swinburne and Dante Gabriel Rossetti were close friends at one time, even briefly sharing a house in London with other artistic friends and hangers-on, though the evidence from Swinburne's correspondence and criticism suggests his indebtedness to the Pre-Raphaelites was not conscious. His possible connections with this English artistic movement bridge at least two of its conflicting streams: the interest in external fact (which he could also have gotten from Gautier), and the fidelity to internal experience which is evident in his poetry and which we have indicated as a possible major P. R. B. influence on Pater.

More significant than Pre-Raphaelite theory, both to Swinburne's own poetic theory and to his practice, and more in line with "l'art pour l'art," law is for Swinburne as for Pater the sine qua non of poetic life. He admits the importance of the personal element in art, but makes no theoretical brief for it as Pater does.[8] As for his own intrusion of personality (perhaps thanks to Pre-Raphaelite tenets of interiority), we know Swinburne best through his poetry. Neither his voluminous correspondence nor his many critical articles reveal the man in the many-sided ways we will see in his poetry. As in the case of Baudelaire, the poet is the man. And with the other advocates of "l'art pour l'art," elitism is also a major consideration for Swinburne. The essay on Blake could hardly be more explicit:

> . . . the sacramental elements of art and poetry are in no wise given for the sustenance or the salvation of men in general, but reserved mainly for the sublime profit and intense pleasure of an elect body or church.[9]

Lesbia Brandon, Swinburne's rambling and probably unfinished novel, contains the most explicit and also highly entertaining denunciations of democracy in favor of elitism. One character constantly denounces democracy and the "illuminated masses," and the book contains a remarkable equation of democracy with nature.

> I fear sometimes that nature is a democrat. Beauty you see is an exception; and excellence means rebellion against a rule, infringement of a law. That is why people who go in for beauty pure and plain--poets and painters . . . are all born aristocrats on the moral side. Nature, I do think, if she had her own way, would grow nothing but turnips; only the force that fights her, for which we have no name, now and then revolts; and the dull soil here and there rebels into a rose. . . . The comfort is that there will always be flowers after us to protest against the cabbage commonwealth and insult the republic of radishes.[10]

Art's purity, poetic law, elitism, art against nature--all this is firmly in the French tradition, with the purist and elitist elements supported also by Pre-Raphaelite attitudes during the movement's later period. What is in neither artistic tradition and what best illustrates the contradictory currents in Swinburne's thought is his view that people have a right to art and that art is nature's highest form.[11] The latter idea can probably be dismissed as simply another attempt to exalt art rather than seen as a fundamental confusion. Swinburne's espousal of the "right to art" raises more serious questions. However vehemently he decries democracy in favor of elitism, Swinburne's poetic themes and ideas of beauty are too universal for the reader to doubt that he saw art's role as something beyond assuaging the sorrows or opening the world only of an elite. He is never the artistocrat of "Perte d'auréole." Furthermore, his lifelong love for children and very old people seems to flow from a poet concerned with the human person in all his complexity and ambiguity.

Swinburne's ideas on beauty vary somewhat from his conceptions of art's role in life, and nowhere is his reliance on the French tradition clearer than here. All the major themes on beauty of the "l'art pour l'art" advocates reappear, almost in identical words. Swinburne is closest to Gautier on the subject of art's role in everyday life. Although Baudelaire also writes of poetry's indispensability, his pose of the dandy makes him far more elitist than Swinburne. Then with all his French counterparts, Swinburne considers spiritual and technical beauty inseparable in art. He criticizes Matthew Arnold as an unsure guide to French poetry in one of his most precocious and influential essays, but in the same essay praises the fusion of spiritual and technical beauty in Arnold's work.

> Success or achievement of an exalted kind on the spiritual side ensures and enforces a like executive achievement or success; if the handiwork be flawed, there must also have been some distortion or defect of spirit, a shortcoming or a misdirection of spiritual supply.[12]

In words which echo Gautier's essay on the beautiful in art and Baudelaire's later praise of Gautier, Swinburne brings together the "l'art pour l'art" themes of beauty's absolute nature, its infinite variety, and the necessity of wordshipping it. "The worship of beauty, though beauty be itself transformed and incarnate in shapes diverse without end, must be simple and absolute."[13]

Swinburne further pursues his ideas of beauty's diverse nature in an 1871 essay on Simeon Solomon, written before his personal falling out with that wretched painter. Swinburne finds that to one interpreter beauty's terror and pity are foremost; to others its shadow, splendor, simplicity or mystery; to others beauty's communion with all things, or its specialty.[14] By this time Swinburne had been strongly influenced by Baudelaire. Although his acquaintance with Les fleurs du mal was only through the expurgated version of 1861, the English poet became a major conduit for Baudelaire's influence in England, and his own ideas of beauty clearly show the intellectual parentage.

Another Baudelairean theme is evident in Swinburne's interest in synesthesia, and his words also echo Gautier. In an essay on Coleridge, Swinburne's comments on "Kubla Khan" paraphrase Baudelaire's "Correspondances": "In reading it we seem rapt into that paradise. . . where music and colour and perfume were one, where you could hear hues and see the harmonies."[15] Perhaps because of his interest in language as music (another part of the "l'art pour l'art" tradition which eventually led to symbolism), Swinburne delighted in writing ballads. He speaks explicitly of language as music. In a letter of 1874, he confesses to delighting in the metrical forms of any language (and he knew Greek, Latin and French well enough to write poetry in them), ". . . simply for the metre's sake, as a new musical instrument."[16] His pleasure is almost childlike when one of his own recent ballads is accepted as authentically medieval.[17]

Also in line with the French tradition, Swinburne shows great interest in ideal beauty and the overripe quality in beauty which Baudelaire exposed so thoroughly. The Chronicle of Tebaldeo Tebaldei, another apparently unfinished work, is intended to illustrate ideal feminine beauty through a study of Lucretia Borgia. As in the case of Lesbia Brandon, Swinburne apparently became involved in a plot so contradictory that he could find no way out and abandoned the attempt. But the fragmentary chapters of the Chronicle provide a fascinating glimpse into some aspects of Swinburne's theories of beauty. The work also demonstrates the immense range of his erudition. He did considerable research into Renaissance Italy for this book, though nowhere does he express such delight with his scholarship as in a letter describing his project of writing the article on Mary Queen of Scots for the Encyclopedia Brittanica.

> . . . it is I, a mere poet, and therefore (as most worthy folk would infer) a naturally feather-headed and untrustworthy sort of person, who am selected to undertake such a responsibility and assume such an authority as a biographer and historian . . . [I am] really gratified and indeed rather elated at such a tribute to my conscientiousness and carefulness, if nothing else.[18]

Unfortunately, however, Swinburne's scholarship takes second place in the Chronicle, along with his interest in ideal beauty, to his fascination with physical pleasure and an unquenchable desire to shock Victorian sensibilities. He claims that beauty is the beginning of all things, then locates all spiritual good in pleasures of the flesh in the rather curious "Treatise on Noble Morals" appended to the work. With Baudelaire he thinks that evil completes good, but that everything is reducible to pleasure. "For in the eyes of the gods, good and evil, gold and brass, are of one value, and go equally to make up pleasure."[19]

Swinburne's emphasis on the value of the corporeal world is similar to Gautier's description of himself as "a man for whom the visible world exists." For Swinburne, too, the visible world is a never-failing source of pleasure, but not in the sense intended by the French "l'art pour l'art" figures. He is far closer to English Romanticism's fascination with nature, speaking of this lifelong delight in an 1895 letter and lamenting the fact that Coleridge and D. G. Rossetti did not take the pleasure in nature which Wordsworth, Tennyson, and he himself experienced. Swinburne thinks if such had been the case, they would have been "much happier" and "much better men."[20] These comments need to be read against the background of Swinburne's conservative and staid years with Watts-Dunton, but they also contain the powerful truth of his own lifetime love of nature. Above all natural phenomena, Swinburne loved the sea. He swam in it with a passion which knew no bounds of physical safety and commented once that he must have been born with the ocean in his veins.[21]

Lesbia Brandon contains the most explicit melding of Swinburne's lyrical interest in the sea, the "l'art pour l'art" theme of overripe beauty, and his personal theme of pleasure derived from pain. The unfinished novel again offers deep insight into Swinburne's theories of beauty. One passage describes his protagonist facing a heavy sea:

> . . . he rioted in the roaring water like a young sea beast, sprang at the throat of waves that threw him flat, pressed up against their soft fierce bosoms and fought for their sharp embraces; grappled with them as lover with lover, flung himself upon them with limbs that laboured and yielded deliciously. . . .[22]

Although the passage is also interesting for its unbridled sexuality, the complex image reveals much about Swinburne's ideas on beauty. The sea becomes a simultaneous image for poetic lyricism, overrripe (almost cloying) beauty, and the pleasure of the flagellant's pain. Still, perhaps for Swinburne, as for his French counterparts, art itself is the greatest pleasure. He claims exactly this: ". . .art . . . always was and is to me the highest, deepest, most precious and serious pleasure to be got out of life."[23]

None of these ideas of beauty or art is original. They do illustrate the lengths to which Swinburne expanded the French "l'art pour l'art" tradition. In place of Baudelaire's fascination with evil and its intersection with good, Swinburne's obsessiveness separates evil from sin and human frailty, thus obscuring its most interesting dimension, its mystery. There is nothing mysterious about his one-dimensional characters in the Chronicle of Tebaldeo Telbaldei or Lesbia Brandon. Nor do his poetic themes come from a world in which evil is many-sided. To Gautier's love of the external world, Swinburne sometimes assents in the extremist fashion of a man for whom this is the only world. And instead of Flaubert's urgings to live for art alone, Swinburne multiplies invective against "Philistia" and the "Puritans." The English poet thus takes a French tradition, translates it almost verbatim into an English vocabulary, but made far more inclusive and negative than the original version when fused with his own personal stridency and placed against the religiosity and utilitarianism of his society.

Side by side with these ideas from the "l'art pour l'art" advocates, Swinburne's poetry offers a contradiction: the traditionalism and universality of its themes. Swinburne speaks to a larger audience, therefore, than we might suppose if we view, for example, only his connections with "l'art pour l'art" or his interest in the Marquis de Sade. There is an implicit role for art in making human life more livable which also emerges from an examination of Swinburne's poetry. Death, time, sorrow, existential longing, and the satiety of human experience are here in abundance. There is surprisingly little in Swinburne's poetry of the English shaper of "l'art pour l'art." Gautier's subjects and Baudelaire's restoration of life's evil face do not have a parallel in his work. On the whole, Swinburne's poetic power evokes far more traditional themes, as in one of his finest lyrical moments in the closing stanzas of "A Ballad of Death."

> Now, ballad, gather poppies in thine hands
> And sheaves of brier and many rusted sheaves
> Rain-rotten in rank lands,
> . . . .
>
> And when thy bosom is filled full thereof
> Seek out Death's face ere the light altereth,
> And say 'My master that was thrall to Love
> Is become thrall to Death."
> Bow down before him, ballad, sigh and groan.

For haply it may be
That when thy feet return at evening
Death shall come in with thee.[24]

Another of Swinburne's poems on death, "The Triumph of Time," has a macabre awareness like Emily Dickinson's of simultaneous consciousness before, during, and after death. Other poems celebrate fate, a major theme in all Swinburne's work. Then there is the pure lyricism of "A Vision of Spring in Winter," echoing themes of loss, time, and sadness.

. . . the hopes that triumphed and fell dead,
The sweet swift eyes and songs of hours that were;
These may'st thou not give back for ever; these
As at the sea's heart all her wrecks lie waste,
Lie deeper than the sea;
But flowers thou may'st, and winds, and hours of ease,
And all its April to the world thou may'st
Give back, and half my April back to me.[25]

And like all weary voyagers, Swinburne seems to long not only for life's revelations but for its rest. Most of his poetry shows a strangely fatalistic quality for a poet who could also apparently celebrate life itself and the immediate reality so vigorously. But Swinburne's is an ambivalent celebration, never far removed from fate and pain. Two other works throw further light on these themes.

Atalanta in Calydon explores life's sadness in the face of inexorable and capricious fate, and Lesbia Brandon once again gives insight into Swinburne's views of art's role in life. Atalanta speaks venomously of the gods' toying with human life, their fashioning madness and sorrow, their destroying anything which might be thought stable. These themes culminate in Swinburne's characterization of "the supreme evil, God."[26] Art provides not only a platform for invective in this remarkable verse drama, but also an escape, a rationale, yet another version of antidote and theodicy. In Lesbia Brandon the pleasure-pain formula which Swinburne finds inseparable from life is analyzed more fully than in any of his other works. Swinburne's protagonist says to his sister at one point, "I wish you would kill me some day; it would be jolly to feel you killing me. Not like it? Shouldn't I! You just hurt me and see."[27] Most eloquently, Margaret exclaims:

> Things in verse hurt one, don't they? hit and sting like a cut. They wouldn't hurt us if we had no blood, and no nerves. Verse hurts horribly; people have died of verse-making, and thought their mistresses killed them--or their reviewers.[28]

There are other psychological insights in Lesbia Brandon. Herbert's pain at being praised for rescuing a drowning boy is oddly mixed with his intense and bitter desire to be praised for something he himself considers important. And Lesbia tells Herbert, "You must be very young. But I wish I knew as much as you; and as little."[29]

Verse is for Swinburne perhaps the ultimate expression of pleasure-pain. Its personal delights for him seem not unlike those he experienced in flagellation, though there are few signs of this in his themes. There are sado-masochistic elements and a little of Gautier's fascination with the hermaphrodite, but Swinburne's basic themes are highly traditional. They carry an implicit meaning that, however deeply verse may hurt, it also makes human existence bearable. Beneath the constructs of "l'art pour l'art," Swinburne's poet is also the redeeming, priestly Romantic reincarnated in the late nineteenth century. But the priest's purpose has changed. Rather than giving access to a sacred world where people can themselves become godlike, the poet's purpose now is the more sinister one of presiding over the death of the gods.

Perhaps for this reason, Swinburne's poetry shows intense appreciation of life's pain, almost anticipating Camus' perception that people do not live long and they are sad. The English poet shares with Baudelaire a sense of time as a ravaging god. Baudelaire speaks of time's infinite cortege of remembrance and regret, Swinburne in "Time and Life" of its elusive, inexorable qualities.

> Time, thy name is sorrow, says the stricken
> Heart of life, laid waste with wasting flame

Ere the change of things and thoughts requicken
Time, thy name.

. . . .

Eyes forspent with vigil, faint and reeling,
Find at last my comfort, and are blest,
Not with rapturous light of life's revealing--
Nay, but rest.[30]

The same themes appear even more hauntingly in "Tiresias":

I prophesy of life, who live with death;
Of joy, being sad; of sunlight, who am blind:
Of man, whose ways are alien from mankind
and his lips are not parted with man's breath;
I am a word out of the speechless years,
The tongue of time, that no man sleeps who hears.[31]

Implicitly, a tone of unachieved desire runs all through Swinburne's poetry. Unlike Pater, for whom art leads to life, ecstasy, and the peak moments, there is no congruence between life and art for Swinburne, and no consummation. Whereas Pater's antidote is to modern fragmentation and Victorian mediocrity, Swinburne's antidote is to time and life itself. In art, he finds his secular version of infinity. Pitting art against life in this way aligns him more firmly with the French "l'art pour l'art" advocates than with Pater. He shares much of the French artists' anti-Enlightenment focus as well. Under the Microscope attacks the scientific preoccupations of his age: "We live in an age when not to be scientific is to be nothing."[32] And in a fine display of his polemical powers, Swinburne derides other intellectual currents of his time:

More is the whole than a part: but half is more than the whole:
Clearly the soul is the body: but is not the body the soul?
One and two are not one, but one and nothing is two:
Truth can hardly be false, if falsehood cannot be true.

. . . .

God, whom we see not, is: and God, who is not, we
 see:
Fiddle, we know, is diddle: and diddle, we take it,
 is dee.[33]

More than any of the other exponents of "l'art pour l'art," Swinburne opposes moralizing. More than even Gautier or Flaubert, he insists that art must exist for itself alone, independent of morality or religion. In opposing all utilitarian implications for art, he also ranges himself with Pater's preference for contemplation over activism. Art is antidote to time, sadness, life, morality, activity. But Swinburne's conceptions of art sometimes push the French theories to the level of shrill polemic, and as such they lose the profundity of the earlier formulations. Even the Victorian middle class could not have been quite so obtuse as Swinburne imagines. His antidote is often reducible to caricature. His theodicy is not.

Swinburne offers the most profound and explicit theodicy of the "l'art pour l'art" tradition. The old gods of belief and superstitution in the Christian dispensation have departed his world; the new deities of utilitarianism, religiosity, and progress are inadequate. Only when all gods have been banished will man be free to make his own destiny. Swinburne explains and justifies the supposed evil in the gods' departure in terms simultaneously modern and quasi-superstitious. The gods themselvs were evil; and human beings are better off without them. By presiding over their demise, the poet makes life more intelligible. The world ought to be desacralized if it is not.

<u>Alalanta in Calydon</u> contains Swinburne's most stinging denunciations of the gods.

For the gods very subtly fashion
 Madness and sadness upon earth:
Not knowing in any wise compassion,
 Nor holding pity of any worth;
. . . .

A little fruit a little while is ours,
        And the worm finds it soon.
But up in heaven the high gods one by one
        Lay hands upon the drought that quickeneth,
Fulfilled with all tears shed and all things and one
        And stir with soft imperishable breath
        The bubbling bitterness of life and death,
And hold it to our lips and laugh; . . .[34]

Swinburne wishes the gods could experience human life, "that they might rise up sad in heaven," and "grieve as men, and like slain men be slain."[35] In the section of his poem which culminates in his denunciations of "the supreme evil, God," Swinburne's invective rises to the pitch of inverted Old Testament prophecy. Man's unachieved desire is the fault of the gods. They must be opposed.

The question arises immediately how seriously this is to be taken. From the entire body of Swinburne's work, we can only conclude that it is meant very seriously indeed. There exist in Atalanta many strands of the French "l'art pour l'art" tradition: Gautier's sense of art as substitute god; Flaubert's realization of the passing nature of belief (which Flaubert himself depicts in St. Antoine's procession of the gods); and even some of the overripe quality of Baudelaire's decadence. Ranged alongside all this and superimposed on an almost-Greek sense of fate, there is the distinctly modern perception that the age of simple belief has ended. For Swinburne, the old gods are not merely dead; they are evil, and that is reason indeed to rejoice in their death.

Other works of the poet underline this view, as Swinburne himself states it, that Dante's god is as dead as Homer's.[36] His poems and letters are replete with this realization. Swinburne takes special pleasure, for example, in his poem "Before a Crucifix," writing to William Rossetti:

> . . . the year 1869 of the Galilean era of superstition . . . I have begun a democratic poem--"Before a Crucifix"--addressed to the Galilean (Ben Joseph) in a tone of mild and modified hostility which I fear and hope will

exasperate his sectaries more than any abuse.[37]

And the poem itself:

This dead God here against my face
     Hath help for no man;

. . . .

The tree of faith ingraffed by priests
     Puts its foul foliage out above thee;
And round it feed man-eating beasts
     Because of whom we dare not love thee;
Though hearts reach back and memories ache;
We cannot praise thee for their sake.

. . . .

     The sun grows haggard at thy name.
Come down, be done with, cease give o'er;
Hide thyself, strive not, be no more.[38]

Swinburne's lines are remarkable for their combination of anger and ache and, from the context of the poem, not only the priests of the past are meant, but all who curse and worship Christ in Swinburne's time.

In other lines, Swinburne laments that no one sees beyond gods and fate. But he is also capable of exulting in human existence when freedom is poised against evil gods and equally evil fate.

Thou art smitten, thou God, thou art smitten; thy
     death is upon thee, O Lord.
And the love-song of earth as thou diest resounds
     through the wind of her wings--
Glory to Man in the highest! for Man is the master
     of things.[39]

All these themes are especially significant because they come from Swinburne's volume Songs before Sunrise, by his own attestation incomparably his best piece of work because "that is a man's best work into which he has put most of his heart and soul and faith and hope."[40]

Swinburne's letters bear out the same themes, though for the great amount of correspondence the poet remains rather hidden. Perhaps the experience of having some of the more salacious segments of early letters publicized during his lifetime by a one-time friend doomed him to greater care in his later correspondence. At any rate, Swinburne speaks frequently enough of fate and the gods, belief and unbelief, Christianity and the Bible, to reinforce the ideas contained in the poetry. Swinburne considers theism an assumption like many other assumptions, reducible finally to the abdication of reason.[41] Yet he seems to have believed in the survival of individual and conscious life after dissolution of the body.[42] Out of the tangle of his religious nonbeliefs and motivations to shock Victorian sensibility, perhaps the final word is Swinburne's own, written in response to a letter from John Ruskin. The poet answers: "You compare my work to a temple where the lizards have supplanted the gods; I prefer an indubitable and living lizard to a dead and doubtful god."[43]

Beneath this there is the tone of the French anti-Faust who can no longer believe either in gods or in human possibility. Even the scattered references to man as master are always in juxtaposition with the gods and fate. Swinburne's art as theodicy explains above all that the gods are the evil creators of madness and sorrow over whose death the poet presides and rejoices. Evil is part of human existence created by the gods, but their defeat through art is inevitable. The poet's entree to a sacred reality is one from which the gods have been expelled. The sacred reality is art which alone frees, heals, and ultimately makes childlike again.

Swinburne's lifelong fascination with children and very old people illuminates yet another aspect of his theodicy. Until the gods can be finally expelled, present evil is made tolerable and justified through primeval innocence, also created by the world of art. The theme of innocence in Swinburne would make a fascinating study. There lingered about him all his life an air of the child, through his early days of post-adolescent delight in shocking his contemporaries to the final years when visitors testified to his eager displaying of books and trophies for the praise a child seeks. His letters contain striking illustrations of his interest in children, well expressed in an 1880 letter: "I don't know how to say what I feel about children--it is as if something of worship was mixed with love of them and delight in them."[44] Swinburne's works evoke a world of innocence, the quality of children and the very old who are unindebted to time and therefore able to approach it without fear.

Swinburne's art restores this world of primeval innocence by expelling the gods who had controlled human destiny. Once the gods have been banished and people freed to manage their own destiny, the sacred realm of art can dare to approach time, death, sadness, and limitation. All these things can be legitimized as parts of human existence (not as the gods' evil work) which art alone makes intelligible and bearable. By making the person complete within himself, through art beyond time and evil, Swinburne also treats art somewhat in the Greek spirit of prophetic malady. His finest poems lead to catharsis, restored unity, stasis. There are glimpses, too, of Gautier's sense of art as play, and through all this the intensely modern spirit of a poet who needs to be separated from the often absurd personal shadow he cast. As surely as his French counterparts, Swinburne conjures art as theodicy and antidote. Art becomes the substitute god in a world stripped of religious pretensions and lacking, as well, a suitable secular religion. Swinburne's reality is thus more aligned with the anti-Faustian French experience than with Pater's world of still-realizable possibility. Although even his finest work is often marred by the shrillness of opposition for its own sake, Swinburne is more modern in his anguished tone than Pater, and as resigned to discontinuity as either Flaubert or Baudelaire. He shares their sense that the Faustian soul is dead and perhaps not even art can fully restore it.

Notes on Chapter VIII

[1]A. C. Swinburne, William Blake (London, 1868), pp. 86 f.

[2]Ibid., p. 89 n.

[3]A. C. Swinburne, "Les fleurs du mal," from The Spectator, September 6, 1862, in Les fleurs du mal and Other Studies, ed. Edmund Gosse, printed for private circulation (London, 1913), pp. 3 f.

[4]A. C. Swinburne, Notes on Poems and Reviews, Under the Microscope, Dedicatory Epistle, ed. Clyde Kenneth Hyder (Syracuse, N.Y., 1966), p. 24.

[5]Ibid., p. 30.

[6]After the nearly fatal physical excesses of his early life, Swinburne lived his last thirty years with his friend Theodore Watts (later Watts-Dunton), who gradually broke his habit of alcoholism. Whether Watts-Dunton also broke Swinburne's spirit has been debated by his biographers. Certainly he became Swinburne's most valued critic, a buffer against friends and enemies alike. The bohemian, iconoclastic poet of the 1860's gradually changed into the conservative figure of the 1890's, though Watts-Dunton did allow Swinburne his visits to a London brothel which catered to his penchant for flagellation. Swinburne's greatest poetry, however, by most accounts belongs to the earlier period of the 1860's and early 1870's.

[7]A. C. Swinburne, Under the Microscope, in Swinburne Replies, p. 77.

[8]A. C. Swinburne, Dedicatory Epistle, in Swinburne Replies, pp. 97, 100.

[9]Swinburne, William Blake, p. 36.

[10]A. C. Swinburne, Lesbia Brandon (London, 1952), pp. 119 f. Also see p. 75 for the discussion of the masses.

[11]To D. G. Rossetti, October 28 [1869], in The Swinburne Letters, ed. Cecil Y. Lang; 6 vols. (New Haven, 1959-62), II, 47. Dates given in brackets are those of the editor.

[12]Swinburne, "Matthew Arnold's New Poems," p. 152.

[13]A. C. Swinburne, "Some Pictures of 1868," Essays and Studies, pp. 379 f.

[14]A. C. Swinburne, "Simeon Solomon's 'Vision of Love,'" from The Dark Blue (July 1871), in Les fleurs du mal and Other Studies, p. 75.

[15]A. C. Swinburne, "Coleridge," Essays and Studies, p. 265.

[16]To E. C. Stedman, February 23, 1874, Swinburne Letters, II, 282.

[17]To Edwin Hatch, September 15, [1858], Swinburne Letters, I, 22.

[18]To Lady Jane Henrietta Swinburne, March 18, 1882, Swinburne Letters, IV, 263.

[19]A. C. Swinburne, "The Treatise of Noble Morals," from The Chronicle of Tebaldeo Telbaldei (publisher's title, Lucretia Borgia (Great Britain, 1942), p. 58.

[20]To Alice Swinburne, December 27, 1895, Swinburne Letters, VI, 94.

[21]To E. C. Stedman, February 20 and 21, 1875, Swinburne Letters, III, 12.

[22]Swinburne, Lesbia Brandon, p. 18.

[23]To D. G. Rossetti, October 28 [1869], Swinburne Letters, II, 47.

[24]A. C. Swinburne, "A Ballad of Death," from Poems and Ballads in Swinburne's Collected Poetical Works, 2 vols.(London, William Heinemann Ltd, 1924) I, 7

[25]A. C. Swinburne, "A vision of Spring in Winter," from Poems and Ballads, Second Series, in Swinburne's Collected Poetical Works, I, 390.

[26]A. C. Swinburne, Atalanta in Calydon: A Tragedy (London, 1889), p. 47.

[27]Swinburne, Lesbia Brandon, p. 81.

[28]Ibid., p. 148.

[29]Ibid., p. 98. See also p. 56 for the drowning incident.

[30]A. C. Swinburne, "Time and Life," from A Century of Roundels, in Swinburne's Collected Poetical Works. II, 535.

[31]A. C. Swinburne, "Tiresias," from Songs before Sunrise, in Swinburne's Collected Poetical Works, I, 837.

[32]Swinburne, Under the Microscope, p. 35.

[33]A. C. Swinburne, "The Higher Pantheism in a Nutshell," from The Heptalogia, in Swinburne's Collected Poetical Works, II, 787.

[34]Swinburne, Atalanta in Calydon, pp. 44 f.

[35]Ibid., p. 45.

[36]A. C. Swinburne, "Recollections of Professor Jowett," Studies in Prose and Poetry (London, 1894), pp. 39 f.

[37]To W. R. Rossetti [November 25, 1869], Swinburne Letters, II, 56 f.

[38]A. C. Swinburne, "Before a Crucifix," from Songs before Sunrise, in Swinburne's Collected Poetical Works, I, 744, 746.

[39]A. C. Swinburne, "Hymn of Man," from Songs before Sunrise, in Swinburne's Collected Poetical Works, I, 764.

[40]To R. H. Stoddard, September 7, 1877, Swinburne Letters, IV, 17.

[41]To William Michael Rossetti, October 26 [1869], Swinburne Letters, II, 44. For other expressions of Swinburne's views on religion, see the letters to John Morley, April 11 [1873], Swinburne Letters, II, 241, and to E. C. Stedman, February 20 and 21, 1875, III, 13 f.

[42]TO William Bell Scott, April 17, 1882, Swinburne Letters, IV, 267.

[43]To John Ruskin, [March 21, 1866?], Swinburne Letters, I, 159 f.

[44]To Lady Jane Henrietta Swinburne, December 22, 1880, Swinburne Letters,IV, 181.

CHAPTER IX

CONCLUSION

Like one of Henri Rousseau's paintings, the artistic world of "l'art pour l'art" presents its own kind of coherence. There was never an artistic school in any formal sense, and the differences among the movement's chief practitioners are as striking as the similarities. What "l'art pour l'art" did was create a world of the anti-Faust, in which neither rationality nor striving prevailed, a world filled with limitation and evil as surely as Rousseau's paintings depict a childlike spirit of play and unnameable terror.

We have examined the theory practiced and expounded by five nineteenth-century writers. For Baudelaire, modernity had rendered the world more unintelligible than ever. A sense of irreparable loss runs through all his work, but it is not a lost god he laments. As the anti-Faust, Baudelaire restores evil. His artistic theories exalt the artificial, the "good" product of human creation juxtaposed with nature's effortless making of evil. Without the foil of evil, the other face of good, neither art nor life makes sense. Human beings are limited and made tragic by time, remembrance, sadness, ultimately by death. If Baudelaire himself was the poet of "L'albatros," life for him was the old saltimbanque, buying resignation at the price of knowing evil. Baudelaire's theodicy justifies evil as the other half of life which he thought his century seemed close to ignoring. His "art for beauty's sake" was antidote to progress, time, rationality, and finally to despair. Just as art cannot exist without evil, life is unlivable separated from art. Of all the poets he might be describing, Albert Béguin's words perhaps fit Baudelaire best: " . . . poetry could be a response, the only possible response, to the fundamental anguish of the creature enclosed within temporal existence."[1]

For Flaubert, too, life was unthinkable without art, the existential solution to the problem of living among the ruins. But Flaubert's focus is on limitation rather than evil. Flaubert's characters live in worlds from which illusion, the irrational and imperfectible half of life, cannot be removed. In a utopia purged of irrationality, there would be neither limitation nor illusion. Flaubert's art preserves both, unassimilated, forever existing on their own terms ready to destroy his characters who deny them, and ready to remind us that we too live in a world ruled by neither progress nor striving. Flaubert's art creates its own illusion of a world set right, not by restoring innocence or good, but by placing limitation, a quasi-evil, in the balance.

Unlike Flaubert, Gautier is the re-enchanter, the creator of alternative worlds. His art begins and ends with illusion, though even within the dream world, evil and limitation exist on their own terms, undissolved into Faustian striving. Gautier is a lesser anti-Faust acquainted with evil and limitation but not their life partner. His art is primarily an antidote to the surface ills of his or any age.

In these three French artists we have met the anti-Faust, a figure in opposition to both Romanticism and the Enlightenment. There is nothing in the theory of "l'art pour l'art" as theory which necessarily implies this anti-Faustian posture. Examined at face value, it is simply a theory of art, highlighting technique, artificiality, synesthesia, and certain aspects of beauty. The social commonality of its main practitioners also appears at first glance to be the desire for an ivory tower of security from the difficulties of their age. Close examination does not totally support either view. "L'art pour l'art" had social meanings far deeper than either artistic theory alone or the creation of an artistic shelter for an elite might imply. "L'art pour l'art" carried an implicit social function hinted at when these writers denounced bourgeois obtuseness, but developed only in the body of their writings where they restore fallibility in the concrete terms of novelistic characters or poetic imagery. Unlike their detractors' ambivalent attitudes toward "decadence," theirs is specified evil and limitation which does not permit dissolution into abstract theories of progress. The ivory tower seems to have functioned as an occasional escape for spirits ultra-sensitive to the pain of their age (and who lived with this constantly in their art) rather than as a retreat from social responsibility. When the Parnassians chose "l'art pour l'art" tenets to justify their own social retreat, they were using a latent factor in the movement for their own purposes.

In the hands of its original practitioners, "l'art pour l'art" was profoundly connected to its century, in spite of Flaubert's protestations of living for art alone, secure in an ivory tower during a barbaric age. In reordering the desacralized world, these French anti-Fausts performed a quasi-religious function, providing new, secular justification for evil and limitation.

An antidote seemed necessary, as well, in mid-nineteenth-century France. Tensions between the society and its intellectuals had exploded under the new pressures of industrialization and democracy which had fundamentally altered the writer's relationship to his society. In this sense, "l'art pour l'art" functioned as an antidote for an artistic elite not yet ready to accept the demands of the marketplace. The body of work produced by these artists also shows that their antidote was to perfectibility and progress, and probably more seriously so. Theirs was simultaneously an anti-Romantic, anti-Enlightenment world. It was also one in which reality could not be explained merely as decadent or progressive, sacred or secular. Justifying evil and limitation as integral to life meant that the human condition itself received a somewhat different explanation. Flaubert's novels and Baudelaire's poetry, perhaps all art, represents a grappling with the intractable. A religiously explained reality could always appear to be less impossible, human life more hopeful, after all. Like all great artists, the French anti-Fausts take illusion, hope, evil, and innocence beyond specifically religious or cultural categories. At the same time, they restore some sense of what the author of Job knew--that evil is indispensable to life, that we start from the fact that perhaps evil is not explainable.

When the "l'art pour l'art" movement migrated across the channel to England, it carried the same theoretical baggage. Swinburne was as interested in art's artificiality as Baudelaire or Gautier. What the theory lacked in England was the same social resonance it found in France where both God and Faust seemed dead, and art could therefore explain evil and limitation, fragments of what had once been the larger Christian ethos. In England the Victorian ethos of religion, stability, and progress continued to a great extent to mask desacralization, accommodating both God and Faust.

But consciousness of desacralization among certain French writers does not necessarily represent a solution. "L'art pour l'art" was not sufficiently encompassing to be any more effective in the long run than either St.-Simonianism or the theory of progress. It was neither secular religion nor social myth. Its role did extend, however, beyond providing solace for a coterie. "L'art pour l'art's" social function was an attempt to give coherence to a society desperately lacking it. As a first step, evil and limitation were restored, theories of progress and perfectibility opposed.

"L'art pour l'art" also furnished a base for future directions in modern art. Its aesthetic legacy is with us today wherever art exists as its own subject. "L'art pour l'art" contributed to modern art's emphasis on the "other-ness" of exterior reality while it explores the very processes of art itself. In Shattuck's apt phrase, the twentieth-century artist stands at the center of a still world revolving around him and indistinguishable from him.

In the absence of generally accepted religious or political bases, the occasional unity our culture shows may stem as much from art as any other source. Fragmentation is one of the many legacies of desacralization, and no new synthesis has yet arisen to replace the Christian consensus unless we accept modernity itself or one of Christianity's own fragmented variants. For our century, too, the problem continues of how to live amid what Flaubert called "the ruins."

Notes to Chapter IX

[1]Albert Béguin, L'Âme romantique et le rêve (Paris, 1946), p. 400.

BIBLIOGRAPHY

The bibliography is arranged according to the following plan: (1) a listing of French and English periodicals consulted; detailed references can be found in the footnotes; (2) primary and secondary materials for Baudelaire, Flaubert, Gautier, Pater, and Swinburne; (3) primary sources on France, England, nineteenth-century art, and art theory; (4) secondary sources on the same. In most cases, collections of works are listed here, with individual citations in the footnotes. Since Gautier's journalistic output is too vast to list individual articles here, the periodicals and newspapers in which he published most frequently are listed at the end of the bibliographical section on Gautier. The footnotes for the Gautier chapter contain details. Because the other four writers' periodical production was smaller, details are given here.

I. Periodicals Consulted

L'Artiste
Figaro
Le Globe
Le Moniteur universel
La Presse
Le Producteur
Revue Contemporaire
Revue des deux mondes
Revue de Paris
Blackwood's Edinburgh Magazine
Contemporary Review
Cornhill Magazine
Dublin University Magazine
Fortnightly Review
Fraser's Magazine
Good Words
Macmillan's Magazine
The Month
The Nineteenth Century
Quarterly Review
Retrospective Review
Westminster Review

II. Baudelaire, Flaubert, Gautier, and Swinburne

a. Baudelaire, primary

Baudelaire, Charles. *L'Art Romantique.* Paris, 1968.

________. *Mon coeur mis a nu*. Paris, 1972.

________. *Correspondance Générale*. Vols. 14-19 of *L'Oeuvres complètes de Charles Baudelaire*. Edited by Jacques Crépet. Paris: Éditions Louis Conard, 1947.

________. *Derniers lettres inédites à sa mère*. Avertissement et notes de Jacques Crépet. Paris, 1926.

________. *Écrits sur l'art*. 2 vols. Paris, 1971

________. *Les fleurs du mal et autres poèmes*. Paris, Libraire Ernest Flammarion, 1964.

________. "Galerie du XIXe siècle": Théophile Gautier. *L'Artiste* 6 (13 mars 1859).

________. *Les paradis artificiels*. Paris, 1961

________. *Petits poèmes en prose: Le spleen de Paris* 1967.

b. Baudelaire, secondary

Bersani, Leo. *Baudelaire and Freud*. Berkeley, 1977.

Decaunes, Luc. *Charles Baudelaire*. Paris, 1965.

Emmanuel Pierre. *Baudelaire: The Paradox of Redemptive Satanism*. Translated by Robert T. Cargo. Birmingham, Alabama, 1970.

Hazard, Paul. *Quatre Études*. New York, 1940.

Klein, Richard J. "Baudelaire and Revolution: Some Notes." *Literature and Revolution*. Edited by Jacques Ehrmann. Boston, 1967.

Messiaen, Pierre. *Sentiment chrétien et poésie française*. Paris, 1947.

Peyre, Henri. *Connaissance de Baudelaire*. Paris, 1951

Sartre, Jean-Paul. *Baudelaire*. Paris, 1963.

Starkie, Enid. *Baudelaire*. Norfolk, Conn., 1958.

Winegarten, Renee. *Writers and Revolution: The Fatal Lure of Action*. New York, 1974.

c. Flaubert, primary

Flaubert, Gustave. "Les arts et le commerce." *Ouevres complètes*. Vol. 12 of 16 vols. Paris: Club de l'Honnête Homme, 1971-75.

________. *Bouvard et Pécuchet*. Including "Dictionnaire des idées reçues." Paris, 1966.

________. *Correspondance*. Vols. 12-16 of *Oeuvres complètes*. Edited by Société des Études littéraires françaises. Paris: Club de l'Honnête Homme, 1971-75.

________. *L'éducation sentimentale.* Paris, 1965.

________. *Madame Bovary*. Paris, 1972.

________. *La Première éducation sentimentale*. Vol. 8 of *Oeuvres complètes*. Paris: Club de l'Honnête Homme, 1971-75.

________. *Salammbô*. Paris, 1970.

________. *La tentation de Saint Antoine*. Paris, 1971.

________. *Trois contes*. Paris, 1973.

d. Flaubert, secondary

Bart, Benjamin. Flaubert. Syracuse, 1967.

Brombert, Victor. Flaubert. "Écrivains de toujours" series. Paris, 1971.

________. The Novels of Flaubert: A Study of Themes and Techniques. Princeton, 1966.

Culler, Jonathan. Flaubert: The Uses of Uncertainty. London, 1974.

Descharmes, René. Flaubert, sa vie, son charactère et ses idées avant 1857. Geneva, 1969.

Sartre, Jean-Paul. L'Idiot de la famille. 3 vols. Paris, 1972.

Starkie, Enid. Flaubert: The Making of the Master. New York, 1967.

________. Flaubert the Master. New York, 1971.

Thibaudet, Albert. Gustave Flaubert. Paris, 1935.

e. Gautier, primary

Bergerat, Émile, ed. Théophile Gautier: entretiens, souvenirs et correspondance. Paris, 1880.

Gautier, Théophile. L'Art moderne. Paris, 1856.

________. "Du beau dans l'art." Revue des deux mondes 19 (1847). Reprinted in Théophile Gautier, L'Art moderne. Paris, 1856.

________. Contes fantastiques. Paris, 1973.

________. Emaux et camées. Paris, 1888

________. L'España de Théophile Gautier Paris, 1929. Édition critique, René Jasinski.

________. Synopsis for "Giselle." Le ballet du Théâtre National de l'Opéra de Paris, 1978.

________. Les grotesques. Paris, 1859.

Gautier, Théophile. Histoire du romantisme. Paris, 1874.

________. Les jeunes france. Paris, 1974

________. Les plus belles lettres de Théophile Gautier présentées par Pierre Descaves. Paris, 1962.

________. Mademoiselle de Maupin. Paris, 1966.

________. Poésies diverses 1833-38. Poésies complètes, vol. I. Paris, 1889.

________. "Préface." Les fleurs du mal. 2nd ed. Paris 1869.

________. "Prospectus." L'Artiste. 14 décembre 1856.

________. Tra los montes: voyage en Espagne. Paris, 1961.

Gautier contributed extensively to the following newspapers and periodicals:

L'Artiste
Le Moniteur universel
La Presse
Revue des deux mondes

f. Gautier, secondary

Giraud, Raymond. "Gautier's Dehumanization of Art." L'Esprit Créateur 3, no. 1 (Spring 1963).

Grant, Richard B. Theophile Gautier. Boston, 1975.

Jasinski, René. Les années romantiques de Théophile Gautier. Paris, 1929.

Richardson, Joanna. _Theophile Gautier: His Life and Times_. London, 1958.

Riffaterre, Michael. "Rêve et réalité dans L'Italia de Théophile Gautier." _L'Esprit Créateur_ 3, no. 1 (Spring 1963).

Smith, James M. "Gautier, Man of Paradox." _L'Esprit Créateur_ 3, no. 1 (Spring 1963).

Tennant, P.E. _Theophile Gautier_. London, 1975.

g. Pater, primary

Pater, Walter. _Appreciations_. London, 1915.

_________. "The Chant of the Celestial Sailors." An unpublished poem. Thirty copies printed by E. H. Blakeney at his private press, 1928.

_________. _Essays from 'The Guardian.'_ London, 1901.

_________. _Gaston de Latour_: _An Unfinished Romance_. London, 1896.

_________. _Greek Studies_. London, 1895.

_________. _Imaginary Portraits by Walter Pater: A New Collection_. Edited by Eugene J. Brzenk. New York 1964.

_________. _Inscription for the Life of Walter Pater_. Winchester: privately printed by E. H. Blakeney, April 1928.

_________. _Letters of Walter Pater_. Edited by Lawrence Evans. Oxford. 1970.

_________. _Marius the Epicurean: His Sensations and Ideas_. 2 vols. London, 1885.

_________. _Miscellaneous Studies_. London, 1899.

_________. _Plato and Platonism_. London, 1893.

_________. "Poems by William Morris." _Westminster Review_ 34 (October 1868).

________. Studies in the History of the Renaissance
London, 1873.

h. Pater, secondary

Cecil, David. Walter Pater the Scholar-Artist. Cambridge, 1955.

Crinkley, Richmond. Walter Pater: Humanist. Lexington, Ky., 1970.

Downes, David Anthony. Victorian Portraits: Hopkins and Pater. New York, 1965.

Fletcher, Ian. Walter Pater. London, 1959.

Gosse, Edmund. "Walter Pater, A Portrait." Contemporary Review 66 (December 1894).

Knoepflmacher, U. C. Religious Humanism and the Victorian Novel: George Eliot, Walter Pater, and Samuel Butler. Princeton, 1965.

de Laura, David J. Hebrew and Hellene in Victorian England: Newman, Arnold, and Pater. Austin, 1969.

Morley, John. "Mr. Pater's Essays." Fortnightly Review 13 (April 1, 1873).

Ward, Anthony. Walter Pater: The Idea in Nature. London, 1966.

Wright, Thomas. The Life of Walter Pater. 2 vols. New York, 1969.

i. Swinburne, primary

Swinburne, Algernon Charles. Atalanta in Calydon: A Tragedy. London, 1889.

________. Ballads of the English Border. Edited by William A. MacInnes. London, 1925.

________. A Century of Roundels, in Swinburne's Collected Poetical Works. 2 vols. London, William Heinemann Ltd, 1924. Vol. 1.

________. The Chronicle of Tebaldeo Tebaldei. (Publisher's title: Lucretia Borgia.) Including "The Treatise of Noble Morals." Great Britain, 1942.

________. Essays and Studies. London, 1875.

________. "Les fleurs du mal." The Spectator, September 6, 1862. Reprinted in Les fleurs du mal and Other Studies. Edited by Edmund Gosse. London: printed for private circulation, 1913.

Swinburne, Algernon Charles. The Heptalogia. Swinburne's Collected Poetical Works. Vol. II. London, 1924.

________. Lesbia Brandon. London, 1952.

________. The Swinburne Letters. Edited by Cecil Y. Lang. 6 vols. New Haven, 1959-62.

________. Poems and Ballads. Swinburne's Collected Poetical Works. Vol. I. London, 1924.

________. Poems and Ballads, Second Series. Swinburne's Collected Poetical Works. Vol. I. London, 1924.

________. Studies in Prose and Poetry. London, 1894.

________. Swinburne Replies: Notes on Poems and Reviews, Under the Microscope, Dedicatory Epistle. Edited by Clyde Kenneth Hyder. Syracuse, 1966.

j. Swinburne, secondary

Fletcher, Ian. Swinburne. Harlow, Essex, 1973.

Fuller, Jean Overton. Swinburne: A Critical Biography. London, 1968.

Henderson, Philip. Swinburne: The Portrait of a Poet. London, 1974.

Lang, Cecil Y. "Introduction." Victorian Poetry 9, nos. 1-2 (Spring-Summer 1971).

Shmiefsky, Marvel. "Swinburne's Anti-Establishment Poetics." Victorian Poetry 9, no. 3 (Fall 1971).

Victorian Poetry 9, nos. 1-2 (Spring-Summer 1971). Special Swinburne issue.

III. Other Primary Sources

About, Edmond. Le Progrès. Paris, 1864.

Aux artistes: Du passé et de l'avenir des beaux-arts (Doctrine de Saint Simon). Pamphlet. Paris 1830.

Bazard, Saint-Armand. Exposition de la doctrine St.-Simonian. 2 vols. Paris, 1830-31.

Bignan, A., Essai sur l'influence morale de la poésie. Paris, 1838.

Caro, E., Études morales sur le temps présent. Paris, 1855

Comte, Auguste. "The Expansion of Sympathy." From The Religion of Humanity, in French Utopias. Edited by Frank E. Manuel and Fritzie P. Manuel. New York, 1971.

Dowden, Edward. Studies in Literature 1789-1877. London, 1878.

Dumas, Alexandre, et al. Paris et les parisiens au XIXe siècle. Paris, 1838.

Dussieux, Louis. L'Art considéré comme le symbole de l'état social. Paris, 1838.

Ellis, Havelock. The Nineteenth Century: A Dialogue in Utopia. London, 1900.

Les français peints par eux-mêmes. 9 vols. Vol. IX: Le Prisme: Encyclopédie morale du dix-neuvième siècle. Paris, 1841.

Froude, J. A. "On Progress," Short Studies on Great Subjects. Edited by David Ogg. London, 1963.

de Goncourt, Edmond, and de Goncourt, Jules. Journal: Memoires de la vie littéraire. 4 vols. Paris, 1959.

Goethe, Johann Wolfgang. Faust, Part One. Translated by Philip Wayne. Middlesex, 1975

________. Faust, Part Two. Bayard Taylor translation. Revised and edited by Stuart Atkins. New York,1962.

Greg, W. R. Literary and Social Judgments. 2 vols. London, 1877.

Houssaye, Arsène. Les confessions: souvenirs d'un demi-siècle 1830-1880. 4 vols. Paris, 1885.

Javary, Auguste. De l'Idée de progrès. Paris, 1851.

Kingsley, Charles. "How To Study Natural History" (1846). Scientific Lectures and Essays. London, 1899.

de Laborde, Léon. De l'union des arts et de l'industrie. 2 vols. Paris: Commission française de l'exposition universelle de Londres, 1856.

de Liefde, C. L. Le saint-simonisme dans la poésie française entre 1825 et 1865. Haarlem, 1927.

Michiels, Alfred. Histoire des idées littéraires en France au XIXe siècle. 2 vols. Paris, 1863.

Mill, John Stuart. Utilitarianism. Edited by Oskar Piest. New York, 1957.

Reade, Winwood. The Martyrdom of Man. London, 1872.

de Saint-Simon, Claude Henri. "The Rule of the Scientists." Letters from an Inhabitant of Geneva to His Contemporaries. In French Utopias. Edited by Frank E. Manuel and Fritzie P. Manuel. New York, 1971.

Smiles, Samuel. Self-Help. London, 1958.

Spencer, Herbert. Social Statics, or the Conditions Essential to Human Happiness. New York, 1969.

Stapfer, Paul. Études sur la littérature française moderne et contemporaine. Paris, 1881.

Wade, John. England's Greatness: Its Rise and Progress in Government, Laws, Religion and Social Life; Agriculture, Commerce, and Manufactures; Science, Literature, and the Arts, from the Earliest Period to the Peace of Paris. London, 1856.

Ward, Thomas Humphrey, ed. The Reign of Queen Victoria: A Survey of 50 Years of Progress. 2 vols. London 1877.

IV. Other Secondary Sources

Abrams, M. H. Natural Supernaturalism. New York, 1971.

Béguin, Albert. L'Âme romantique et le rêve. Paris, 1946.

Best, Geoffrey. Mid-Victorian Britain 1851-1875. London, 1971.

Bevington, Merle Mowbray. The Saturday Review 1855-1868: Representative Educated Opinion in Victorian England. New York, 1941.

Briggs, Asa. The Age of Improvement 1783-1867. New York, 1959.

________. Victorian People. Chicago, 1970.

Buckley, Jerome Hamilton. The Triumph of Time: A Study of the Victorian Concepts of Time, History, Progress, and Decadence. Cambridge, Mass., 1967.

________. The Victorian Temper: A Study in Literary Culture. London, 1966.

Bury, J. B. The Idea of Progress. New York, 1932.

Carter, A. E. The Idea of Decadence in French Literature 1830-1900. Toronto, 1958.

Cassagne, Albert. La théorie de l'art pour l'art en France chez les derniers romantiques et les premiers réalistes. Paris, 1906.

Chadwick, Owen. The Secularization of the European Mind in the Nineteenth Century. Cambridge, 1975.

________. The Victorian Church. 2 vols. London, 1970.

Charlton, D. G. Secular Religions in France 1815-1879 London, 1963.

Clark, T. J. The Absolute Bourgeois: Artists and Politics in France 1848-1851. Greenwich, Conn., 1973.

Cruickshank, John, ed. French Literature and Its Background. 6 vols. Vol. IV: The Early Nineteenth Century. Vol. V: The Late Nineteenth Century. London, 1969.

Egan, Rose Frances. "The Genesis of the Theory of 'art for art's sake' in Germany and in England." Smith College Studies in Modern Languages (Part I) 2, no.4 (July 1921); (Part II) 5, no. 3 (April 1924).

Estève, Edmond. Byron et le romantisme français. Paris, 1907.

Evans, David Owen. Social Romanticism in France 1830- 1848. Oxford, 1951.

Everett, Edwin Mallard. The Party of Humanity: The Fortnightly Review and Its Contributors 1865-1874. Chapel Hill, 1939.

Gaunt, William. The Aesthetic Adventure. London, 1975.

George, Albert Joseph. The Development of French Romanticism: The Impact of the Industrial Revolution on Literature. Bruges, 1955.

Girard, René. Deceit, Desire, and the Novel: Self and Other in Literary Structure. Translated by Yvonne Freccero. Baltimore, 1965.

Graña, Cesar. Bohemian versus Bourgeois. New York, 1964.

Green, F. C. A Comparative View of French and British Civilization 1850-1870. London, 1965.

Guérard, Albert. Art for Art's Sake. Boston, 1936.

_________. "Art for Art's SAke." Southwest Review 59, no. 4 (1974).

Halévy, Elie. England in 1815. New York, 1961.

_________. The Liberal Awakening 1815-1830. New York, 1961.

Heller, Erich. The Artist's Journey into the Interior. New York, 1965.

_________. The Disinherited Mind. London, 1971.

Hemmings, F. W. J. Culture and Society in France 1848-1898. New York, 1971.

Herbert, Eugenia. The Artist and Social Reform: Belgium, 1885-1898. New Haven, 1961.

Himmelfarb, Gertrude. Victorian Minds. New York, 1968.

Hobsbawm, E. J. The Age of Revolution 1789-1848. New York, 1962.

_________. Labouring Men: Studies in the History of Labour. New York, 1964.

Hough, Graham. The Last Romantics. Oxford, 1961.

Houghton, Walter E. The Victorian Frame of Mind 1830-1870. London, 1957.

Lanson, Gustave. Histoire de la littérature française. Paris, 1952.

Lowenthal, Leo. Literature, Popular Culture, and Society. Englewood Cliffs, 1961.

McLeod, Hugh. Class and Religion in the Late Victorian City. London, 1974.

Moore, Barrington, Jr. Social Origins of Dictatorship and Democracy. Boston, 1966.

Ortega y Gasset, Jose. "The Dehumanization of Art." In The Dehumanization of Art and Other Essays on Art,Culture, and Literature. Princeton, 1968.

Otto, Rudolf. The Idea of the Holy. Translated by John W. Harvey. New York, 1970.

Pankhurst, Richard K. P. The Saint Simonians Mill and Carlyle: A Preface to Modern Thought. London, 1957.

Poggioli, Renato. The Theory of the Avant-Garde. Cambridge, 1968.

Rosenblatt, Louise. L'Idée de l'art pour l'art dans la littérature anglaise pendant la période victorienne. Paris, 1931.

Schaffer, Aaron. Parnassus in France: Currents and Cross-Currents in Nineteenth Century French Lyric Poetry. Austin, 1929.

Shattuck, Roger. The Banquet Years: The Origins of the Avant Garde in France: 1885 to World War I. New York, 1968.

Schenk, H. G. The Mind of the European Romantics. Garden City, 1969.

Seaman, L. C. B. Victorian England: Aspects of English and Imperial History 1837-1901. London, 1973.

Simon, Walter M. "History for Utopia: Saint-Simon and the Idea of Progress." Journal of the History of Ideas 17 (June 1956).

Starkie, Enid. From Gautier to Eliot: The Influence of France on English Literature 1851-1939. London, 1960.

Stokoe, F. W. German Influence in the English Romantic Period 1788-1818. New York, 1963.

Stone, Lawrence Social Change and Revolution in England 1540-1640. London, 1965.

Swart, Koenraad W. The Sense of Decadence in Nineteenth Century France. The Hague, 1964.

Temple, Ruth Zabriskie. The Critic's Alchemy: A Study of the Introduction of French Symbolism into England. New York, 1953.

Tholfsen, Trygve R. Working Class Radicalism in Mid-Victorian England. New York, 1977.

Thompson, E. P. The Making of the English Working Class. New York, 1963.

van Tieghem, Paul. Le romanticisme dans la littérature européene. Paris, 1948.

Watt, Ian. The Rise of the Novel. Berkeley, 1957.

Wearmouth, R. F. Methodism and the Working Class Movements of England 1800-1850. London, 1937.

Wellek, René. A History of Modern Criticism 1750-1950. 5 vols. Vol. IV: The Later Nineteenth Century. New Haven and London, 1965.

Whitehead, Alfred North. Science and the Modern World. Cambridge, 1927.

Wilcox, John. "The Beginnings of L'art pour l'art." Journal of Aesthetics and Art Criticism 11, no. 4 (June 1953).

Williams, Roger L. Gaslight and Shadow: The World of Napoleon III: 1851-1870. New York, 1957.

Williams, Raymond. Culture and Society 1780-1950. New York, 1966.

Young, G. M., ed. Early Victorian England 1830-1865. 2 vols. London, 1934.

Young, G. M. Portrait of an Age. London, 1960.

Zeldin, Theodore. France 1848-1945. 2 vols. Vol. I: Ambition, Love, and Politics. Oxford, 1973.